COUNTRIES
OF THE
WORLD

WITHDRAWN

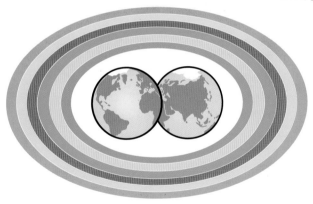

KINGFISHER
NEW YORK

KINGFISHER
LONDON & NEW YORK

Text and design copyright © Toucan Books Ltd. 2018
Illustrations copyright © Simon Basher 2018
www.basherbooks.com

Published in the United States by Kingfisher,
175 Fifth Ave., New York, NY 10010
Kingfisher is an imprint of Macmillan Children's Books, London.
All rights reserved.

Consultant: Kimberly Weir
Text written by Mary Budzik
Maps © Cosmographics Ltd.

Dedicated to Kas & Leigh, Ella & Jos, Anais, Manon & Lou

Distributed in the U.S. and Canada by Macmillan,
175 Fifth Ave., New York, NY 10010

Library of Congress Cataloging-in-Publication Data has been applied for.

PB ISBN: 978-0-7534-7379-5
HB ISBN: 978-0-7534-7378-8

Kingfisher books are available for special promotions and premiums.
For details contact: Special Markets Department, Macmillan,
175 Fifth Avenue, New York, NY 10010.

For more information, please visit www.kingfisherbooks.com

Printed in China
9 8 7 6 5 4 3 2 1

1TR/0618/HH/UG/128MA

Contents

Introduction

Step into Basher's world and meet the characterful countries of the United Nations (UN), all jostling for space across the globe's continents. The UN is an international organization with roots in World War II. A "country," meanwhile, is any region that is run by its own government. The idea is that countries belonging to the UN try to avoid warfare and do all they can to make sure their people have equal rights and opportunities. That's what the countries have in common with each other. This book, on the other hand, considers the things that make them distinct. So let's find out what they're all about.

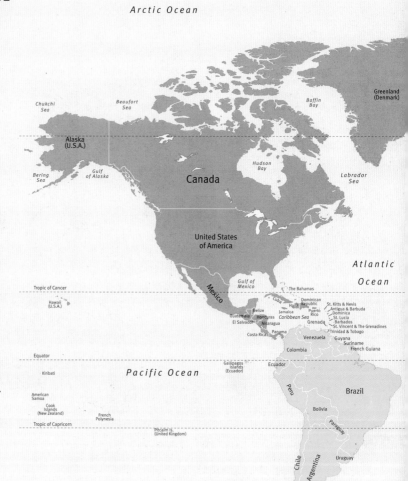

Look for this symbol throughout the book.
It shows the capital city of each country.

North America

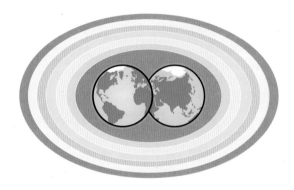

'm no kid. Some of my rocks are the oldest in the world—four billion years old to be exact! And I can be extreme at times . . . after all, you'll find 57,660 square miles (149,340 sq km) of land ice in Canada, while Death Valley in the United States holds the record for the highest temperature recorded on Earth (134°F/57°C, in 1913). But my 23 countries are one big melting pot!

People have come from all over the world to make my homelands their home, bringing their own cultural flavors. It doesn't hurt that much of my topography is roomy and well watered. Complex river systems and huge lakes help keep the land fertile for agriculture and support the wonderful creatures that inhabit my lush forests—from the subarctic north to the tropical south.

- ☀ **Land mass:** 9,540,000 sq mi (24,709,000 sq km)
- ☀ **Number of countries:** 23

- ☀ **Biggest lake:** Superior
- ☀ **Longest river:** Mississippi
- ☀ **Highest mountain:** Denali

North America

Antigua & Barbuda

Bahamas, The

Barbados

Belize

Canada

Costa Rica

Cuba

Dominica

Dominican Republic

El Salvador

Grenada

Guatemala

Haiti

Honduras

Jamaica

Mexico

Nicaragua

Panama

St. Kitts & Nevis

St. Lucia

St. Vincent &
The Grenadines

Trinidad & Tobago

United States of America

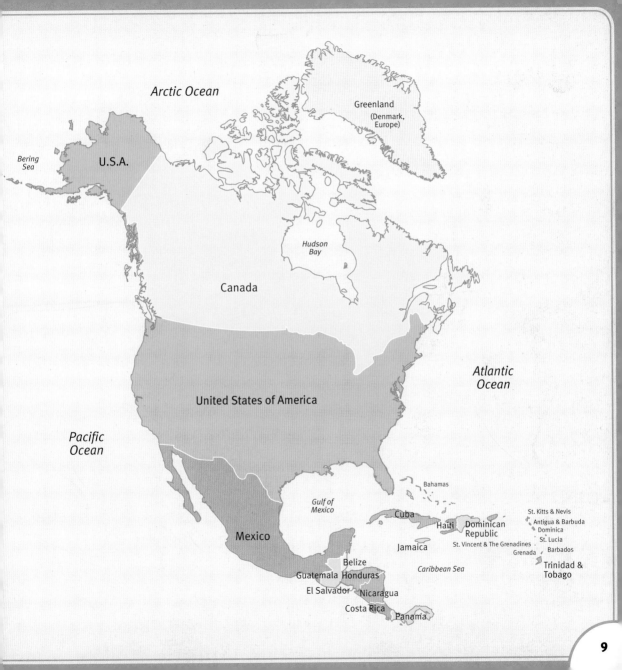

Arctic Ocean

Greenland
(Denmark,
Europe)

Bering
Sea

U.S.A.

Hudson
Bay

Canada

Atlantic
Ocean

Pacific
Ocean

United States of America

Bahamas

Gulf of
Mexico

Cuba

St. Kitts & Nevis
Antigua & Barbuda
Dominica

Mexico

Haiti

Dominican
Republic

Jamaica

St. Lucia

St. Vincent & The Grenadines

Grenada

Barbados

Belize

Caribbean Sea

Trinidad &
Tobago

Guatemala Honduras

El Salvador

Nicaragua

Costa Rica

Panama

United States of America

NORTH AMERICA

* The capital, Washington, D.C., is home to the president's residence—the White House
* New York's Statue of Liberty is one of the country's best-known sights
* The cable cars in San Francisco are the only historic landmarks in the U.S. that move

I'm so large and diverse, everybody dreams of getting to know me, but how? Start up high, I say! Scale my heights for city views—from Chicago's Willis Tower to San Francisco's Transamerica Pyramid. Or clamber up mountains mighty (the Rockies) and old (the ancient, eroded, coal-pitted Appalachians).

Take a grand tour, beginning down south in the Florida Everglades, my largest tropical wilderness, or visit the Mississippi Delta, once the haunt of bluesmen. Channel the writer Mark Twain by taking a riverboat down the Mississippi River. Canter on a paint horse across the desert to the Four Corners—the arid, rugged point on the Colorado Plateau where New Mexico, Colorado, Arizona, and Utah meet. But show respect—this is Navajo territory: After the Cherokee of my Southeast, the Navajo are my second-largest native tribe. Step onto the glass floor of the Grand Canyon Skywalk, 2000 feet (610 m) aboveground, or try your luck with a roll of the dice at Las Vegas. Heading north to my buffalo-roaming plains, stop in South Dakota to see my monumental rock sculptures: first, legendary Sioux chief Crazy Horse, and farther east, four presidents carved into the side of Mount Rushmore. Peckish? Finish up in corn-growing Iowa, home to the country's oldest popcorn factory.

- **SIZE:** 3,796,742 sq mi (9,833,517 sq km)
- **POPULATION:** 323,996,000
- **CURRENCY:** U.S. dollar
- **CAPITAL:** Washington, D.C.
- **LANGUAGE:** English

Charters of Freedom

Three documents have shaped the laws of this country and influenced the rights of its citizens: The Declaration of Independence, the Constitution, and the Bill of Rights (the first ten amendments to the Constitution).

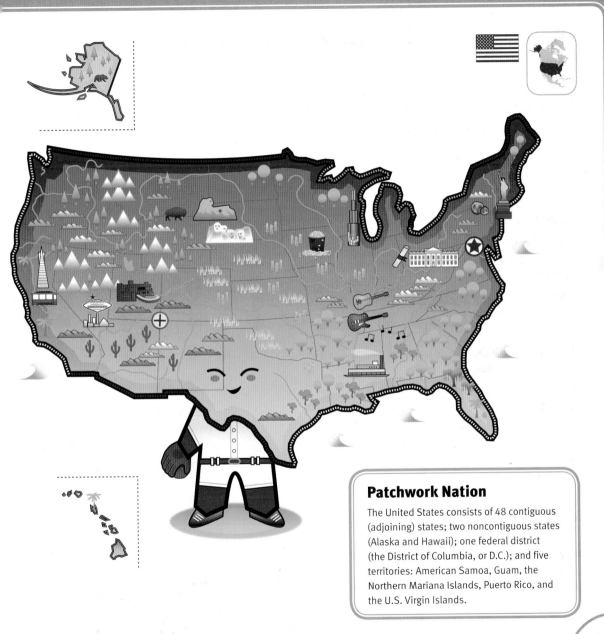

Patchwork Nation

The United States consists of 48 contiguous (adjoining) states; two noncontiguous states (Alaska and Hawaii); one federal district (the District of Columbia, or D.C.); and five territories: American Samoa, Guam, the Northern Mariana Islands, Puerto Rico, and the U.S. Virgin Islands.

Canada

NORTH AMERICA

- British Columbia's Kootenay National Park includes both glaciers and cacti
- A town in Alberta built a municipal landing pad for extraterrestrial spaceships
- Poutine—French fries and cheese curds covered in gravy—is a popular Canadian dish

Chilled! That's me. A no-drama kind of country—unless my ice hockey teams aren't doing well, of course. I'm the world's second-largest country in area, but my entire population is less than LA and New York combined. Eighty percent of my people live within 60 miles (100 km) of the U.S. border—the world's longest international frontier! Just check out my territory—it covers four biomes, or ecosystems. From my north, the Arctic chilly, treeless tundra gives way to dense conifer forest. South of here, where it is slightly warmer, more deciduous trees grow and the forest runs into rolling prairies. You can imagine the wildlife—from polar bears to deer, hawks, and wolves. Out west, the Rocky Mountains cut through British Columbia; lying to my south the Great Lakes (Superior, Michigan, Huron, Erie, and Ontario) form the world's largest group of freshwater lakes.

For centuries, my indigenous people traveled in canoes and on dog-powered sleds. These days, folk are more likely to take the 4990-mile (8030-km) Trans-Canada Highway to get from A to B. Crossing all ten provinces from Pacific to Atlantic, it connects all my major cities. In Québec, don't be fooled into thinking you're in France; it was a French colony for more than 200 years, and French is still widely spoken.

- **SIZE:** 3,855,103 sq mi (9,984,670 sq km)
- **POPULATION:** 35,363,000
- **CURRENCY:** Canadian dollar
- **CAPITAL:** Ottawa
- **LANGUAGES:** English, French

First Nations

The indigenous population of Canada includes Inuits, Native Indians, and Métis (those with European and Indian ancestry). Today, these groups account for around one million people.

Tar Sands

Bitumen: sounds like spitting, but is so much more valuable. My midwestern province, Alberta, has the world's largest deposit of this heavy, semisolid petroleum— unrefined oil. It is formed from the decayed organic matter of an ancient sea that covered the area around the time of the dinosaurs.

Mexico

NORTH AMERICA

* The ancient Olmecs carved massive stone heads—some as tall as 11 feet (3 m)
* Parícutin, one of the world's youngest volcanoes, emerged as recently as the 1940s
* Corn originated in Mexico more than 7000 years ago

Imagine this: life without chocolate, corn, or chili peppers. That's right, I introduced those delights to the world. I've been here for millennia—long before the Spanish explorer Hernán Cortéz arrived in 1519.

From skinny northwestern Baja California to the Yucatán peninsula in my southeast, I manage to squidge no fewer than nine geographic regions between my Atlantic and Gulf of Mexico coasts—that's no mean feat. Expect to see the Rio Grande and Colorado Rivers, arid coastal plains, scorching deserts, lush mesas (flat-topped hills), and volcanic mountains. More? Sure. How about touristy Acapulco beaches, a Copper Canyon, and a limestone karst riddled with sinkholes. Oh, and I have resources a-plenty: silver, lead, zinc, copper, tin, and oil.

My people go back a long, long way. The Olmec civilization from my south lays claim to being the earliest in the Americas (around 1200 B.C.E.). Succeeding the Olmecs, were the Mayans, Aztecs, and Toltecs, among other awesome civilizations. Mexico City, my great contemporary capital, was established on the ruins of Tenochtitlán, the ancient Aztec capital that was thriving in 1519 . . . until Hernán Cortéz burned it down.

SIZE: 758,449 sq mi (1,964,375 sq km)

POPULATION: 123,167,000

CURRENCY: Mexican peso

CAPITAL: Mexico City

LANGUAGE: Spanish

Play Ball!

The Olmecs invented the rubber ball and used it to play *tlachtli*, a game that was a little like basketball (get the ball through a ring) and a little like soccer (no hands). Losers were sacrificed to the gods!

Hernán Cortéz

Hernán Cortéz was the Spanish conquistador who led an expedition to Mexico, shortly after the country's discovery by Europeans in the early 1500s. Although the Aztec leader, Montezuma, showered Cortéz with gifts, relations soon soured. Battles ensued and eventually brought an end to the Aztec Empire.

Belize

NORTH AMERICA

* Sugar, bananas, and citrus fruits are among Belize's main exports
* Part of the Belize Barrier Reef, the Great Blue Hole is the largest sinkhole in the world

My species tickle your tongue and strike sparks in your eyes . . . trees include allspice, calabash, frangipani, and soursop. I count the tapir, margay, and gibnut among my animals. And my national flower is the black orchid—sounds like it could slay you, no?

I sit on the east coast of Central America. My northern territory is all limestone lowlands and swamps. Toward the south, I rise up to the rugged Maya Mountains, with Victoria Peak their highest point. Dense jungle fills my interior and the Belize Barrier Reef, the world's second-longest, lies just off my shores. Mayans inhabited me from 1500 B.C.E.— their legacy is the ancient site of Caracol in my Cayo District. Millennia later, European settlers known as Baymen established logging colonies to harvest my logwood tree. Its extracts are used for dye and to indicate acid levels for medical tests. In 1840, I was colonized by British people searching for mahogany wood in my dense forests—they left the English language as their legacy.

● **SIZE:** 8867 sq mi (22,966 sq km)
● **POPULATION:** 354,000
● **CURRENCY:** Belizean dollar
● **CAPITAL:** Belmopan
○ **LANGUAGES:** English, Spanish, Creole

Guatemala

NORTH AMERICA

I'm popping with volcanic mountains, earthquakes, and Caribbean coastal hurricanes! In the jungle lies the ancient Mayan city of Tikal. One kind of forest wasn't enough for me: I've got mangrove, cloud, rain, and pine. Even my animals specialize—in names with intense spelling: try *phyllomedusa*, quetzal, and jaguarundi. I stay chilled by chomping gum: One of my exports is *chicle*, sapodilla tree sap used to make chewing gum.

- **SIZE:** 42,042 sq mi (108,889 sq km)
- **POPULATION:** 15,190,000
- **CURRENCY:** Guatemalan quetzal
- **CAPITAL:** Guatemala City
- **LANGUAGES:** Spanish, Amerindian

El Salvador

NORTH AMERICA

Notched into the Isthmus of Panama, I'm the smallest, most densely populated Central American country. If I am not suffering storms at the hands of El Niño, I'm quaking in seismic fear of volcanic activity. My ancient city of Joya de Cerén bears witness to this and is likened to Italy's Pompeii. Other features include my coffee plantations and the beloved sea turtles—four of the world's eight species—who've made me their home.

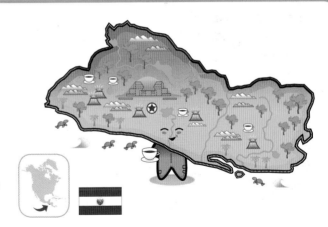

- **SIZE:** 8124 sq mi (21,041 sq km)
- **POPULATION:** 6,157,000
- **CURRENCY:** U.S. dollar
- **CAPITAL:** San Salvador
- **LANGUAGE:** Spanish

Honduras

NORTH AMERICA

* The mountains in Honduras make up 80 percent of the country's terrain
* Mahogany used for Gibson guitars is sustainably logged in the Honduran rain forest

- **SIZE:** 43,278 sq mi
  (112,090 sq km)
- **POPULATION:**
  8,893,000
- **CURRENCY:**
  Honduran lempira
- **CAPITAL:**
  Tegucigalpa
- **LANGUAGE:**
  Spanish

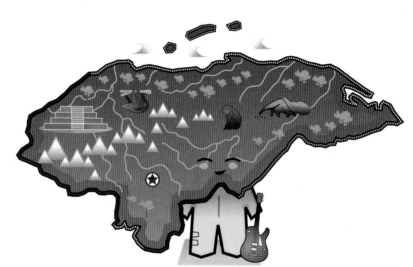

Christopher Columbus himself named me. In 1502, on his final voyage, he landed on my Caribbean coast and noticed the waters were unusually deep. *Honduras* means "depths" in Spanish, hence my name.

I'm almost completely surrounded by water, with the Caribbean Sea to the north and the Pacific Ocean to the south. More than half of my border with Nicaragua consists of water—the Coco River. Inland from Mosquito Coast, once home to the Mosquito Indians, my Río Plátano Biosphere Reserve is a whopping 3260 miles (5250 km) of rain forest, roamed by the mantled howler monkey, the giant anteater, and the brown-throated sloth. Elsewhere, my forests of pine and oak have been logged for growing bananas and coffee—major exports of mine. Close to my border with Guatemala lies the ancient Mayan city, Copán.

Nicaragua
NORTH AMERICA

✹ Nicaragua's northern tamandua looks like an anteater wearing a panda-bear coat

✹ Agricultural crops include corn, beans, plantains, and cassava

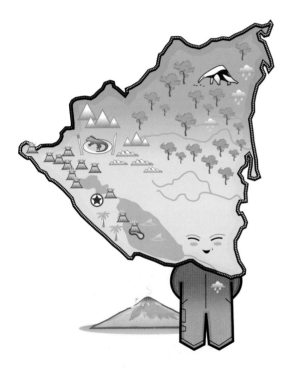

I am Central America's largest country and my northeastern coastline gets the most rainfall in the whole region. Having said that, in times of drought—as a water-saving tip—my people are advised to keep and eat iguanas instead of chickens. Yum!

Take it from the pirates who loved me—I'm a tropical hotspot—literally. My earth bubbles with volcanic energy. To my west, nineteen active volcanoes form a belching, boiling chain from northwest to southeast. That's not all bad; I'm working on harnessing their energy to give my people access to geothermal power, and the weathering of volcanic ash makes my soils rich and fertile. Besides volcanoes, I'm known for my lakes. Lago de Nicaragua, my enormous interior lake, boasts as many as 365 islets, two volcanic islands (Ometepe and Zapatera), and even the occasional bull shark! In the olden days, the lake was connected to the Pacific by a stagecoach line run by Cornelius Vanderbilt, an American tycoon!

○ **SIZE:** 50,366 sq mi (130,370 sq km)

○ **POPULATION:** 5,967,000

○ **CURRENCY:** Nicaraguan córdoba

● **CAPITAL:** Managua

○ **LANGUAGE:** Spanish

Costa Rica

NORTH AMERICA

Check out my numbers! I occupy 0.03 percent of Earth's surface, but contain six percent of its biodiversity. And I am committed to preserving that environment; hydroelectric plants generate four-fifths of my electricity. I enjoy a tropical climate and six of my fourteen volcanoes are active. Not fiery enough for you? Check your sandals before putting them on—when my bullet ants bite, the pain rivals that of a gunshot.

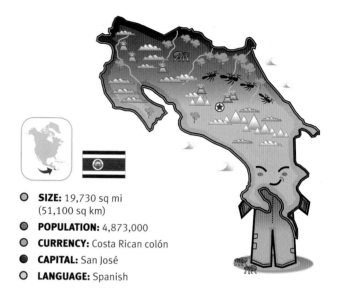

- **SIZE:** 19,730 sq mi (51,100 sq km)
- **POPULATION:** 4,873,000
- **CURRENCY:** Costa Rican colón
- **CAPITAL:** San José
- **LANGUAGE:** Spanish

Panama

NORTH AMERICA

See my skinny waist, the Isthmus of Panama? Its canal (built in 1914) makes for a great shortcut between the Atlantic and Pacific Oceans. Mountains form my spine, while dense tropical forest makes up 40 percent of my land. Hundreds of unique species thrive there, including my national flower, a white orchid called Flor del Espíritu Santo (Flower of the Holy Spirit). Oh, and with more than 500 rivers, I'm no stranger to hydroelectric power.

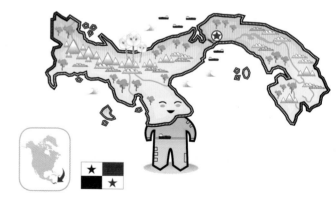

- **SIZE:** 29,120 sq mi (75,420 sq km)
- **POPULATION:** 3,705,000
- **CURRENCY:** Panamanian balboa, U.S. dollar
- **CAPITAL:** Panama City
- **LANGUAGE:** Spanish

Cuba

❋ Cuba is home to classic dance styles that include the mambo and cha-cha-chá

❋ Baseball is the favorite sport of Cuban people

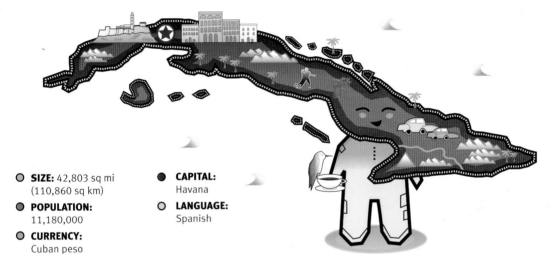

- **SIZE:** 42,803 sq mi (110,860 sq km)
- **POPULATION:** 11,180,000
- **CURRENCY:** Cuban peso
- **CAPITAL:** Havana
- **LANGUAGE:** Spanish

Separated from Key West, Florida, by a 100-mile (160-km) strait, I'm the largest island in an archipelago that is also called Cuba. My mountainous coastlines give way to a mostly flat terrain, dotted with limestone hills.

Before Columbus arrived in 1492, the indigenous Taino and Ciboney tribes occupied my land. Spanish colonizers set up sugar and coffee plantations, and my port of Havana was where ships departed for Spain, laden with New World riches. Today, Havana harbor is guarded by a turreted fortress built to scare away pirates. Since my Communist revolution of 1958, modernization has been minimal, and today I feature classic old buildings painted in Easter egg colors and lovingly maintained 1950s American cars. My 300 native birds species include the world's smallest—the bee hummingbird.

Dominican Republic

NORTH AMERICA

I make up half of Hispaniola Island—the better half, obviously, since I'm the most visited island in this sea. Even Christopher Columbus stopped by, in 1492. Do people come to see the Caribbean's tallest mountain (Pico Duarte) and its largest lake (Enriquillo)? Or perhaps they are attracted by my year-round golf courses? I like to think the lure is my lively music, *merengue típico*, which features the *güira*—a perforated metal scraper played with a brush.

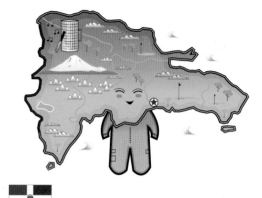

- **SIZE:** 18,792 sq mi (48,670 sq km)
- **POPULATION:** 10,607,000
- **CURRENCY:** Dominican peso
- **CAPITAL:** Santo Domingo
- **LANGUAGE:** Spanish

Haiti

NORTH AMERICA

The smaller half of Hispaniola, I was once a French colony and the New World's richest. In 1801, I became the first New World country to abolish slavery. Since then, hurricanes have blown and earthquakes rumbled across my mountainous terrain, yet my people walk tall (balancing water jugs on their heads). My brightly painted homes show my cheerful spirit, while the practice of voodoo gave rise to the legend of zombies.

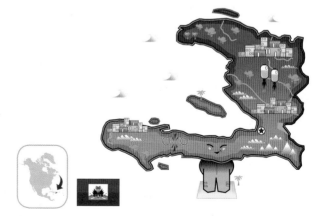

- **SIZE:** 10,714 sq mi (27,750 sq km)
- **POPULATION:** 10,486,000
- **CURRENCY:** Haitian gourde
- **CAPITAL:** Port-au-Prince
- **LANGUAGES:** French, Haitian Creole

Jamaica
NORTH AMERICA

✳ At the Hope Botanical Gardens you can see the blue mahoe, Jamaica's national tree
✳ Jamaica's giant swallowtail is the western hemisphere's largest swallowtail butterfly

○ **SIZE:** 4244 sq mi (10,991 sq km)
◑ **POPULATION:** 2,970,000
○ **CURRENCY:** Jamaican dollar
● **CAPITAL:** Kingston
○ **LANGUAGES:** English, Jamaican Patois

Lying 90 miles (145 km) south of Cuba, I'm an island crossed from east to west by the forested Blue Mountains that are famous for their high-quality coffee.

I've got a lilt all my own, a beat as jaunty as my percussive reggae, and a flavor that's as sweet, hot, and bubbly as my ginger beer. You see, African slaves created my culture. Imported by my Spanish and English colonizers to work on sugar, cocoa, and coffee plantations, through agitation and escape they made me their own and created a culture with African roots and Caribbean flavor. Today, I've got a vibrant music culture and an eye-opening cuisine: Mannish water, a stew, is made with all parts of the goat (including feet). The ackee, my national fruit, is only for the initiated: Eat the wrong parts, and you might get Jamaican Vomiting Sickness.

The Bahamas

NORTH AMERICA

A British colony since 1783, I didn't gain my independence until 1973—the Brits are gone, but cricket is here to stay. An Atlantic archipelagic state, I consist of 700 islands, cays (low islands), and islets. *Bahamas* means "shallow water" in Spanish; the differences in depth of sea around my cays (reflected in its colors) can be seen in photos from space. Be sure to go to the island of Great Inagua—home to some 50,000 flamingos, my national bird.

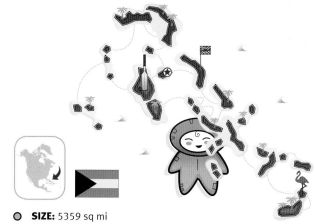

- **SIZE:** 5359 sq mi (13,880 sq km)
- **POPULATION:** 327,000
- **CURRENCY:** Bahamian dollar
- **CAPITAL:** Nassau
- **LANGUAGE:** English

Antigua & Barbuda

NORTH AMERICA

A dorable twin islands, we've been an independent state within the British Commonwealth since 1981. Known for our intricate coastlines, we are said to have 365 beaches—one for each day of the year. Sadly, the good life we offer is threatened by sea-level rise and drought—the two of us are short of rivers, lakes, and streams. A number of our species are at risk too, including the yellow-breasted Barbuda warbler.

- **SIZE:** 170.9 sq mi (442.6 sq km)
- **POPULATION:** 94,000
- **CURRENCY:** East Caribbean dollar
- **CAPITAL:** St. John's
- **LANGUAGES:** English, Antiguan Creole

Barbados

NORTH AMERICA

* You can take a tour of 1.5-mile- (2.4-km-) long Harrison's Cave by tram
* The blind, burrowing Barbados threadsnake is about the size of a quarter

I'm sweet! That's me alright, oozing sugar and molasses since the British arrived in 1627. I'm situated in the western North Atlantic, northeast of Venezuela; my British colonial history is evident in the cricket greens and Episcopalian churches that dot my villages. My name means "bearded ones"—figure that out! The name likely refers to the aerial roots of my native bearded fig tree, which resemble bundles of grizzled, gray hair hanging beneath the foliage.

Mostly flat, I'm composed of coral-reef limestone (or sediments deposited over centuries by decayed sea-creature skeletons) and am riddled with caves—85 of them, in fact. Animal Flower Cave, my only sea cave, features sea anemones that disappear into stalks when threatened. Compared to nearby islands, I have few endemic, or native, species—that's partly due to people introducing non-natives that take over, and partly because I am younger than my neighbors. My only truly native mammals are bats!

○ **SIZE:** 166 sq mi (430 sq km)

○ **POPULATION:** 291,000

○ **CURRENCY:** Barbadian dollar

○ **CAPITAL:** Bridgetown

○ **LANGUAGES:** English, Bajan

Dominica

NORTH AMERICA

* Columbus named the island for the day on which he discovered it—Sunday (in Italian)
* Dominica's biggest exports are bananas and soap

A mountainous isle of rain forests, natural hot springs, sulfur vents, and a boiling lake, I've got a full head of steam. Located between the Caribbean and the North Atlantic along with Guadeloupe and Martinique, I became the last Antilles island to be settled by Europeans, because my native Kalinago (Carib) people put up a good fight. The Kalinago called me Waitukubuli—"tall is her body"—because of my steeply ridged, forested terrain. Despite colonization, my Carib people live on—the only remaining pre-Columbian population in the entire Caribbean. Way to go, guys!

Be warned! You'll not catch a tourist bus to my Boiling Lake in the Morne Trois Pitons National Park; instead, embark on a mucky hike through the fumarole-ridden Valley of Desolation. My carnival showcases original folk music developed by descendants of the West African slaves. Expect such sounds as jing ping, bouyon, and a dance known as the flirtation.

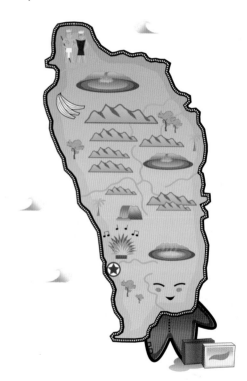

- **SIZE:** 28,478 sq mi (73,757 sq km)
- **POPULATION:** 74,000
- **CURRENCY:** East Caribbean dollar
- **CAPITAL:** Roseau
- **LANGUAGES:** English, Dominican Creole

Grenada

NORTH AMERICA

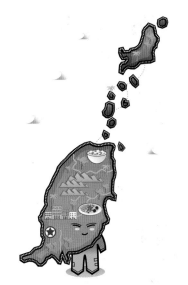

I'm a diddy little island chain whose capital nestles neatly in a natural harbor. Pretty, pastel-colored houses rise up the hillsides from the sea. I'm known as "spice island": Pantries far and wide are stocked with the nutmeg, allspice, and ginger that flourish here due to my climate, rainfall, and volcanic ash-enriched soil. Chocolate, too. Oil Down, my national dish, is a stew of breadfruit and meat seasoned with the yellow spice turmeric.

- ○ **SIZE:** 133 sq mi (344 sq km)
- ◑ **POPULATION:** 111,000
- ○ **CURRENCY:** East Caribbean dollar
- ● **CAPITAL:** St. George's
- ○ **LANGUAGES:** English, Grenadian Creole

St. Kitts & Nevis

NORTH AMERICA

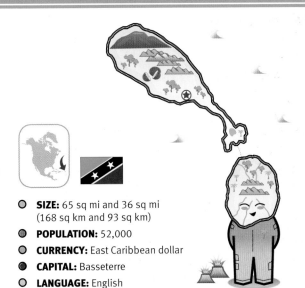

Two volcanic islands in one sovereign state, we are separated by 2 miles (3 km) of water. We happen to major in coconuts. Small and round, Nevis amounts pretty much to the sum of its only mountain, Nevis Peak. The more shapely St. Kitts has a ridge of volcanoes down its back; the highest—Mount Liamuiga—has a lake in its crater. The two of us sit in a tropical hurricane zone. Things get wet and windy between August and October.

- ○ **SIZE:** 65 sq mi and 36 sq mi (168 sq km and 93 sq km)
- ◑ **POPULATION:** 52,000
- ○ **CURRENCY:** East Caribbean dollar
- ● **CAPITAL:** Basseterre
- ○ **LANGUAGE:** English

St. Lucia

NORTH AMERICA

I have subterranean minerals, gases, and mud that refuse to stay put. That's right, I'm home to Sulfur Springs, otherwise known as the "drive-in" volcano: You can walk right through the crater. Heat from deep in Earth's core bubbles up through my steam vents. Luckily, the blue-headed, red-breasted, green-backed jacquot—my native parrot—prefers to perch in my interior rain forest, a safe distance from any boiling potholes.

- **SIZE:** 238 sq mi (616 sq km)
- **POPULATION:** 164,000
- **CURRENCY:** East Caribbean dollar
- **CAPITAL:** Castries
- **LANGUAGES:** English, French Patois

St. Vincent & The Grenadines

NORTH AMERICA

Blessed or cursed? You decide. My Carib natives called me Hairouna, "Land of the Blessed." My volcanic soil is so rich, it's said a pencil would sprout and grow in it, but a volcano's blessings are mixed: In 1902, an eruption killed 1680 people. King's Hill Reserve in Kingstown is the western hemisphere's oldest botanic garden; it was established after a drought, on the assumption that preserving trees would increase rainfall.

- **SIZE:** 150 sq mi (389 sq km)
- **POPULATION:** 102,000
- **CURRENCY:** East Caribbean dollar
- **CAPITAL:** Kingstown
- **LANGUAGES:** English, Vincentian Creole

Trinidad & Tobago
NORTH AMERICA

✳ Endangered leatherback sea turtles use Trinidad's Matura Beach as a nesting site
✳ Calypso music and steel-drum bands originated in Trinidad & Tobago

We're siblings, so we love to tease. Just ask us! Trinidadians will say that Tobagans are too serious. Tobagans will say that Trinidadians need to stop shaking to a calypso beat and get in line. But we love each other, really—you can call us Trinbago!

Trinidad lies just 7 miles (11 km) off the Venezuelan coast—its Northern Range of mountains is simply a continuation of the Andes. Down south, thanks to gas and water seepage (euch!) the island is known for its mud volcanoes. Tiny Tobago carries the Andes even farther, its Main Ridge sloping down to sugarcane-growing plains. We love red around here! You can't miss the clear reddish-orange of Trini's national bird, the scarlet ibis, or the evil red sting of the scorpion—the Trinidad Moruga pepper that is officially the world's hottest. Cool your tongue with our purple-red sorrel drink, distilled from roselle, a kind of hibiscus flower. Have a glass and *lime* with us—that's Trinbago speak for "hanging out."

⦿ **SIZE:** 1980 sq mi (5128 sq km)
⦿ **POPULATION:** 1,220,000
⦿ **CURRENCY:** Trinidad and Tobago dollar
⦿ **CAPITAL:** Port of Spain
⦿ **LANGUAGE:** English

South America

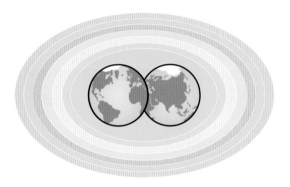

Does any other continent match my geographical wealth? From my belly full to the brim with the fat Amazon rain forest to my tiny, island-studded tip named for flames—Tierra del Fuego—I am a continent bursting with tremendous vitality. Even the textiles produced by my indigenous people are fabulously colorful! You may say I'm boastful, but the fate of the world could depend on me.

Think about it: One-fifth of the world's oxygen is produced in my rain forest. Charles Darwin, father of the science of evolution, formed his theory of the natural selection of species after visiting my Galápagos Islands. Even my deserts are chart-topping: Outside of Antarctica, Chile's Atacama Desert, in the rain shadow of my Andes Mountains, is the driest nonpolar place on Earth.

* **Land mass:** 6,890,000 sq mi (17,840,000 sq km)
* **Number of countries:** 12

* **Biggest lake:** Maracaibo
* **Longest river:** Amazon
* **Highest mountain:** Aconcagua

South America

Argentina

Bolivia

Brazil

Chile

Colombia

Ecuador

Guyana

Paraguay

Peru

Suriname

Uruguay

Venezuela

Caribbean Sea

Venezuela

Colombia

Guyana

Suriname

French
Guiana

Ecuador

Peru

Brazil

Bolivia

Paraguay

Chile

Pacific
Ocean

Uruguay

Argentina

Atlantic
Ocean

Venezuela

SOUTH AMERICA

* Anacondas, the world's largest snakes, live in the Orinoco River basin
* General Rafael Urdaneta Bridge, named for a war hero, is 5.4 miles (8.7 km) long

○ **SIZE:** 352,144 sq mi
(912,050 sq km)

◉ **POPULATION:**
30,912,000

○ **CURRENCY:**
Venezuelan bolivar

◉ **CAPITAL:**
Caracas

○ **LANGUAGE:**
Spanish

I know all about steep drops, thanks to Angel Falls, the world's highest uninterrupted waterfall. Another drop—in the price of oil—hasn't worked out for me, though. That viscous liquid should be my fortune. My Orinoco Belt contains the largest proven oil reserves in the western hemisphere, but low prices combined with my government's mismanagement have left many of my people facing poverty.

Thankfully, my natural strengths don't fail me. In my northwest, Lake Maracaibo is South America's largest lake. In my center, more than 2000 tributaries riddle my Orinoco River basin. Running across my interior, the Guiana Highlands underpin the largest undamaged tropical rain forest in the world. And then there is Mount Roraima. This *tepui*, or tabletop mountain, marks a triple border point for me, Guyana, and Brazil.

Guyana
SOUTH AMERICA

I was once a colony of the Netherlands, which explains the name of my city, New Amsterdam, famous for its mission chapel. But who needs the city life, when most of my land is forested? Stroll on a treetop walkway in my Iwokrama rain forest; safe from the jaguars below, you might spot a toucan. Rivers flow here, too. My Demerara River gave its name to the colony that founded my thriving sugarcane industry—mmm, those sweet crunchy crystals.

- **SIZE:** 83,000 sq mi (214,969 sq km)
- **POPULATION:** 736,000
- **CURRENCY:** Guyanese dollar
- **CAPITAL:** Georgetown
- **LANGUAGES:** English, Guyanese Creole

Suriname
SOUTH AMERICA

I'm the only Dutch-speaking country in South America (once I was a colony of the Netherlands). I'm small, but fiery! Every *Oud Jaar* (Old Year, but actually New Year), ribbons and ribbons of red firecrackers snap, crackle, and sizzle in my capital. My two mountain ranges give way to rain forest and savanna; Tafelberg, a heavily forested, waterfall-rich mesa, is probably full of undiscovered plant and animal species.

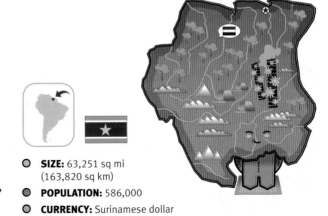

- **SIZE:** 63,251 sq mi (163,820 sq km)
- **POPULATION:** 586,000
- **CURRENCY:** Surinamese dollar
- **CAPITAL:** Paramaribo
- **LANGUAGE:** Dutch

Colombia

SOUTH AMERICA

- Ciudad Perdida ("Lost City") dates from 800 C.E. and contains 200 structures
- Andean spectacled bears inhabit Puracé National Natural Park

I'm in chains! Three parallel longitudinal chains of the Andes Mountains, called *cordilleras*, stretch across me diagonally north to south. Known as the Occidental (Western), Central, and Oriental (Eastern) cordilleras, they feature peaks as high as 18,700 feet (5700 m). Bogotá, my capital, perches on a plateau in the Oriental cordillera; at 9190 feet (2800 m), it's the third-highest capital in the world.

East of the mountains, rain forests and plains dominate my territory, covering about three-fifths of my total area. But jungles aren't the only green around here: I am the world's largest source of emeralds, especially the prized Trapiche gemstones found only in mines on the western side of the Eastern cordillera. And finally, wait for it . . . I'm bicoastal! There's the Caribbean to my north and the Pacific Ocean out west. It's on my Caribbean coast that you'll find the walled city and fortress of Cartagena—the continent's most strongly fortified city.

- **SIZE:** 439,736 sq mi (1,138,910 sq km)
- **POPULATION:** 47,221,000
- **CURRENCY:** Colombian peso
- **CAPITAL:** Bogotá
- **LANGUAGE:** Spanish

Peru

SOUTH AMERICA

* The once-lost Inca city of Machu Picchu sits up high in the Andes Mountains
* Cerro Blanco in Nazca is the highest sand dune in the world

With more than 90 different microclimates, I'm hard to pin down weather-wise, but I can promise you this: Visit me, and 4000 varieties of potato, yellow underpants, and roasted guinea pig (including feet!) will be yours to enjoy.

The details: I'm situated in western South America, with a coastal plain bordering the Pacific, the Andes Mountains inland, and the Amazon Basin to the east of the Andes. The Norte Chico civilization on my arid, north-central coast is the oldest known civilization in the Americas—thriving around 3500 B.C.E. (the same time the Egyptians were building the Pyramids). About the guinea pig: Called "*cuy*," it's a traditional Andean dish, as are potatoes of every color and stripe. Andean Indians became the first to domesticate the potato by selective breeding: The wild plant is toxic. Without them, the world would be French-fry-less. Yellow underpants? Any self-respecting Peruvian street stall sells them at New Year; they're considered good luck.

- **SIZE:** 496,225 sq mi (1,285,216 sq km)
- **POPULATION:** 30,741,000
- **CURRENCY:** Peruvian sol
- **CAPITAL:** Lima
- **LANGUAGES:** Spanish, Quechua, Aymara

Ecuador

SOUTH AMERICA

Let's set a few things straight. First, Mount Everest may have the highest elevation, but my Mount Chimborazo is the world's tallest when measured from Earth's core. And Panama hats? Sure, first sold in Panama, but made by Ecuadorean artisans! Country with the world's greatest biodiversity per square mile? Yeah, me. World's largest exporter of bananas? Me. Only country named for the Equator (which actually runs through me)? All me, me, me!

- **SIZE:** 109,484 sq mi (283,561 sq km)
- **POPULATION:** 16,081,000
- **CURRENCY:** U.S. dollar
- **CAPITAL:** Quito
- **LANGUAGE:** Spanish

Chile

SOUTH AMERICA

Long, slender, and slinky, I'm the narrowest country in the world, lining South America's Pacific coast from Peru to Cape Horn. What can I tell you? My Atacama Desert is the driest place on Earth. My earthquakes often hit 9.5 on the Richter scale. And Gran Abuelo, a native Fitzroya tree of mine, is 3622 years old. Meanwhile, on my remote Easter Island in the southeastern Pacific, big-headed statues represent the godlike ancestors of the Rapa Nui people.

- **SIZE:** 291,933 sq mi (756,102 sq km)
- **POPULATION:** 17,650,000
- **CURRENCY:** Chilean peso
- **CAPITAL:** Santiago
- **LANGUAGE:** Spanish

Bolivia
SOUTH AMERICA

- ✳ La Paz has the world's highest seat of government (11,975 feet/3650 m above sea level)
- ✳ People dressed in zebra suits work as road-crossing guards

Deep underground, in shafts and tunnels, that's where you'll find my story. Colonial rulers exploited my veins of silver and tin—and my indigenous peoples—for centuries. Cerro Rico, Potosí's rich mountain, was known as the mountain that eats men, but now it's eating itself. It's been so heavily mined that its peak is caving in. Still, my people have ways to resist: They turn to El Tio, a devilish god who guards the mines.

Aboveground, my Salar de Uyuni, the world's largest salt flat, is so reflective it's used to calibrate satellites from space. Take care not to stray into its forest of giant cacti! These spiky types grow slowly—just ½ inch (1 cm) a year—but reach heights of 39 feet (12 m). Ouch! My Altiplano is the world's most extensive high plain outside Tibet. The pink flamingos here are real, not lawn ornaments, and chinchillas are rodents, not coats. And Bolivian women always express their independent style with a gracious tip of their bowler hats!

- ○ **SIZE:** 424,164 sq mi (1,098,581 sq km)
- ○ **POPULATION:** 10,970,000
- ○ **CURRENCY:** Bolivian boliviano
- ● **CAPITAL:** La Paz (administrative), Sucre (constitutional)
- ○ **LANGUAGES:** 36 official languages, including Spanish, Quechua, and Aymara

Brazil

SOUTH AMERICA

* Taking up half the continent of South America, Brazil is more than 50 percent rain forest
* Brazil's soccer team has qualified for every World Cup to date and has won five times
* Rio de Janeiro's Statue of Christ the Redeemer is one of Brazil's best-known landmarks

Let's face it. Big and resource rich, I am a match for any of the big world players—and not just in the soccer stadium. The fifth-largest country in the world by area *and* population, I cover four time zones and border all other countries in South America . . . well, apart from Ecuador and Chile!

I've got beaches, rain forests, and most of the Amazon River. The Pantanal at my center is the world's largest tropical wetland. You'll see jaguars, toucans, caimans, and many other species here. But I'm not all wilderness and jungle. My two biggest cities, Rio de Janeiro and São Paulo, are humongous, too.

Did I mention my resources? Once the Portuguese "discovered" me in around 1500 C.E., it was game on. Initially, the Europeans exploited my Pau Brasil tree (yes, I'm named for a tree!), but that tree signified just the beginning. In the 17th century, explorers discovered emeralds and gold in my Minas Gerais region. After that, over 30,000 pounds (13,600 kg) of gold a year was exported to Europe. Two of my most important exports, coffee and rubber, dominated the 19th century—especially after Charles Goodyear found a way to make my natural rubber durable enough to make automobile tires, in 1844.

○ **SIZE:** 3,287,957 sq mi (8,515,770 sq km)

● **POPULATION:** 205,824,000

○ **CURRENCY:** Brazilian real

● **CAPITAL:** Brasília

○ **LANGUAGE:** Portuguese

Carnival

Every year, street parties take over Brazil's cities at the start of Lent. The most famous happens in Rio de Janeiro, where people dress up and dance in the streets to the steady beat of drums.

Woody Emblem

The Pau Brasil is the country's national tree. *Pau* means "wood" in Portuguese and *Brasil* comes from the Portuguese word for "ember"; the reddish wood of the tree, resembling embers, yielded a valuable red dye and the wood is prized for the bows used to play stringed instruments.

Paraguay

SOUTH AMERICA

From north to south, I'm sliced right down my center by the Paraguay River, my lifeblood. I use its mighty force to create hydroelectric power (and lots of it). I'm also a producer of "green gold" (soy)—the world's fourth-largest producer, in fact. To relax, I get caught up in the vivid colors of *ñandutí* (spiderweb) lace-making, or craft vibrant feather capes and headdresses like the ones worn by my native shamans.

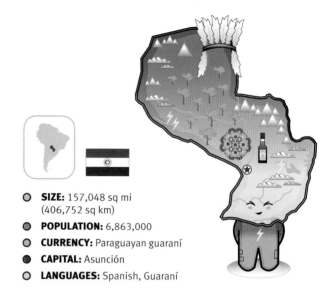

- **SIZE:** 157,048 sq mi (406,752 sq km)
- **POPULATION:** 6,863,000
- **CURRENCY:** Paraguayan guaraní
- **CAPITAL:** Asunción
- **LANGUAGES:** Spanish, Guaraní

Uruguay

SOUTH AMERICA

Located on the south Atlantic between Argentina and Brazil, my high point is the curious Cerro Catedral (Cathedral Hill). Otherwise, I'm rocking, rolling pampas (plains) where cows outnumber people. My name means "river of painted birds" for the migrating flocks that fly over my long coastal lowlands. We like herbs here: Yerba maté tea sipped through a bombilla (straw), from a gourd (hollowed-out fruit) thermos, is my national drink.

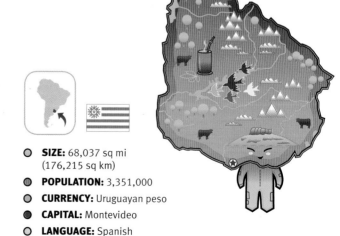

- **SIZE:** 68,037 sq mi (176,215 sq km)
- **POPULATION:** 3,351,000
- **CURRENCY:** Uruguayan peso
- **CAPITAL:** Montevideo
- **LANGUAGE:** Spanish

Argentina
SOUTH AMERICA

* Elephant seals, fur seals, penguins, and sea lions swim off the coast of Patagonia
* Gauchos, like American cowboys, symbolize the open plains of the Pampas region

Sink or soar—you choose! The options? Well, you can rise up to Aconcagua, in my western Andes; this "sentinel of stone" is the highest mountain in the western hemisphere. Or you can sink down to Laguna del Carbón, a salt lake in cold, arid Patagonia that also happens to be the lowest point in the western hemisphere. I like extremes, you see; just take my tango, a ballroom dance that originated in the Buenos Aires slums.

Hired assassins! That's what my polo players are called when they play overseas. They perfected their game on my southwestern pampas, home to more hard riders: my *gauchos* (cowboys). Seeking more thrills? Why not speedboat under Iguazú Falls—with 275 cataracts, they are twice as tall and three times wider than Niagara! Or head to the Valdes Peninsula in Patagonia for a spot of whale-watching. And you can always dip your toes into the Atlantic at Tierra del Fuego. This "fiery land" is the archipelago at the southernmost point of the Americas.

○ **SIZE:** 1,073,518 sq mi (2,780,400 sq km)

○ **POPULATION:** 43,887,000

○ **CURRENCY:** Argentine peso

● **CAPITAL:** Buenos Aires

○ **LANGUAGE:** Spanish

Europe

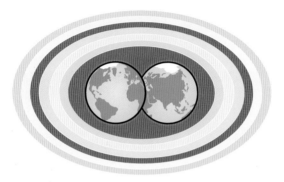

Pack 'em in! I rank third in continental population and contain 45 countries. My people are famous as sailors—to satisfy their wanderlust, they had to take to ships. Starting with the Vikings, their seafaring prowess is legendary! At home, my people consoled themselves with castles—turreted towers teetering on crags and magnificent moated manor houses in ancient fairy-tale forests.

Try mapping my coastlines: With peninsulas and fjords, islands and inlets, channels, firths, and forths, there's not a straight line to be seen! I've also known some colossal collisions in my time: My Alpine mountains are an ancient continental pileup, the rocky wreckage left behind when the European and African tectonic plates crashed into each other millions of years ago.

- ❋ **Land mass:** 3,930,000 sq mi (10,180,000 sq km)
- ❋ **Number of countries:** 45

- ❋ **Biggest lake:** Ladoga
- ❋ **Longest river:** Volga
- ❋ **Highest mountain:** Mont Blanc

Europe

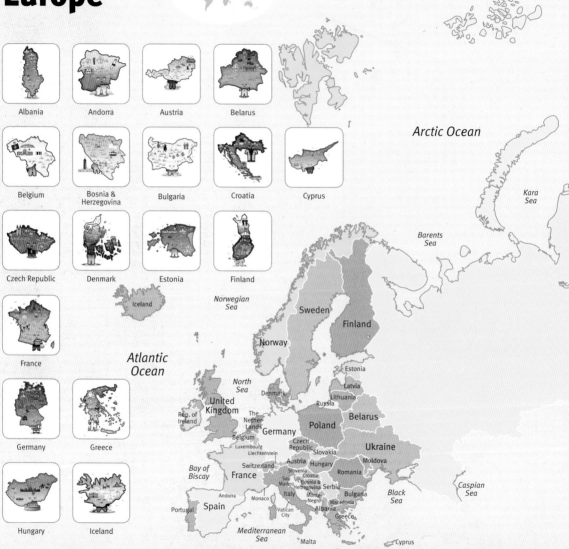

Albania

Andorra

Austria

Belarus

Belgium

Bosnia & Herzegovina

Bulgaria

Croatia

Cyprus

Czech Republic

Denmark

Estonia

Finland

France

Germany

Greece

Hungary

Iceland

Arctic Ocean

Kara Sea

Barents Sea

Norwegian Sea

Iceland

Atlantic Ocean

Sweden

Finland

Norway

Estonia

North Sea

Denmark

Latvia

Lithuania

United Kingdom

Russia

Rep. of Ireland

The Netherlands

Germany

Poland

Belarus

Belgium

Luxembourg

Czech Republic

Ukraine

Liechtenstein

Slovakia

Moldova

Switzerland

Austria

Hungary

Bay of Biscay

France

Slovenia

Croatia

Romania

San Marino

Bosnia & Herzegovina

Serbia

Andorra

Monaco

Italy

Monte Negro

Bulgaria

Black Sea

Caspian Sea

Portugal

Spain

Vatican City

Macedonia

Albania

Greece

Mediterranean Sea

Malta

Cyprus

Ireland, Republic of

Italy

Latvia

Liechtenstein

Lithuania

Luxembourg

Macedonia

Malta

Moldova

Monaco

Montenegro

Netherlands

Norway

Laptev Sea

Poland

Portugal

Romania

Russia

Bering Sea

San Marino

Russia

Sea of Okhotsk

Pacific Ocean

Serbia

Slovakia

Slovenia

Spain

Sweden

Switzerland

Ukraine

United Kingdom

Vatican City

Iceland

EUROPE

* Icelanders must choose a baby's name from a government-approved list
* Eight percent of Icelanders believe in mythical *huldufólk* ("hidden people," or elves)

○ **SIZE:** 39,769 sq mi
(103,000 sq km)

● **POPULATION:**
336,000

○ **CURRENCY:**
Icelandic króna

● **CAPITAL:**
Reykjavík

○ **LANGUAGE:**
Icelandic

My name says it all! When I was first inhabited, foxes were the only other land mammals roaming my icy terrain. Over the millennia, humans also introduced farm animals, reindeer, and mink.

I sit smack on top of the Mid-Atlantic Ridge, where the North American and Eurasian tectonic plates hitch up . . . except they're splitsville—at the rate of ¹/₁₀ in (2.5 mm) a year.

That's right, I'm slowly being pulled apart by continental drift. My geology suffers the occasional temper tantrum, due to its geysers, hot springs, and volcanoes. In 2010, I gave most of Europe a piece of my mind and sent forth a cloud of volcanic ash that grounded airline flights across the continent. I'm not all about mayhem, though. The Althing, my parliament, was founded in 930 C.E.—it's the world's oldest legislature. Sooo civilized!

Denmark

- Denmark's royal family has reigned uninterrupted for over 1000 years
- Pigs outnumber humans in Denmark, by as many as four to one

I have a playful streak: My countrypeople invented LEGO® and I'm home to the Tivoli Gardens, one of the world's oldest amusement parks. Among my most famous sons is Hans Christian Andersen—storyteller extraordinaire. Who hasn't read his moral tales of vain emperors, little mermaids, and ugly ducklings?

Even my shape is whimsical: I'm a peninsula with an archipelago of 406 islands, and I'm surrounded by the North Sea, Baltic Sea, Kattegat Strait, Skagerrak Strait, and (if you count my territories of Greenland and the Faroe Islands), the North Atlantic and Arctic. You'd need an Excel spreadsheet to keep track of my natural harbors. Nowhere am I less than 30 miles (48 km) from the sea, and I have 7314 miles (11,770 km) of coastline. Oh yes, I love bridges: The Great Belt links my islands of Zealand and Funen, while the Øresund Link connects my capital to Malmö in Sweden. I'm even connected to Germany by bridge (and land, and—soon—underwater tunnel). Not bad for the smallest country in Scandinavia, eh?

SIZE: 16,639 sq mi (43,094 sq km)

POPULATION: 5,594,000

CURRENCY: Danish krone

CAPITAL: Copenhagen

LANGUAGE: Danish

Norway

EUROPE

* Oslo's Viking ship museum features a real Viking ship excavated from a burial mound
* On average, Norway's children spend 16.9 years in school

I'm more than the naked eye can see. Specifically, the part of my landmass that unfurls under the sea—my continental shelf—is four times the size of my dry land. In the 1970s, geologists discovered vast deposits of natural gas and oil beneath my seabed. Thanks to that, my citizens enjoy free healthcare, free education, and the highest standard of living in Scandinavia. My coastline is feathered by hundreds of islands, islets, and bays. No surprise, then, that I am rich in fish and support the largest fishing industry in Europe.

Ancient glaciers carved a landscape of fjords ringed by craggy cliffs. It must be all the *lutefisk* (codfish soaked in lye) and lingonberries they eat, but my people have exploration in their bones. Ever since the Vikings, they've been known for it. In 1911, Norwegian explorer Roald Amundsen led the first expedition to the South Pole, and Fridtjof Nansen was the first person to sail across the Arctic Ocean. *Tusen takk* ("Thanks!"), guys, you make me proud!

- **SIZE:** 125,021 sq mi (323,802 sq km)
- **POPULATION:** 5,265,000
- **CURRENCY:** Norwegian krone
- **CAPITAL:** Oslo
- **LANGUAGE:** Norwegian

Sweden

EUROPE

- Sweden's Riksbank, founded in 1668, is the world's oldest national bank
- At August's crayfish festivals, the crustaceans are cooked in beer and topped with dill

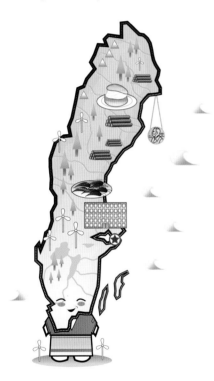

Bursting with natural resources, much of my land is forest, and logging accounts for at least 10 percent of all my industry. I'm steeped in minerals, too. Four elements in the periodic table take their names from just one village, Ytterby: erbium, terbium, yttrium, and ytterbium. I'm especially rich in uranium, which is used as a fuel in nuclear power plants. But I have a conscience: I tax nuclear power, subsidize wind power, and was the first country to establish an Environmental Protection Agency. Alfred Nobel showed similar concern. This native of Stockholm invented dynamite, but wanted to leave a less explosive legacy, so endowed the Nobel Prizes for excellence in the arts and sciences.

Anyone fancy a *semla*? My national treat, these wheat buns are stuffed with almond paste and cream. And kids, if you snatch one rudely from the plate, you won't get your hand slapped. In 1979, I outlawed corporal punishment, leading the world in this humane legislation!

○ **SIZE:** 173,860 sq mi (450,295 sq km)
○ **POPULATION:** 9,880,000
○ **CURRENCY:** Swedish krona
● **CAPITAL:** Stockholm
○ **LANGUAGE:** Swedish

51

Finland

EUROPE

☀ Watch the northern lights in Lapland from the comfort of a heated glass igloo

☀ Finns love to take a sauna—a type of steam bath—it's their way of life

I am Europe's most sparsely populated country and share my northern Lapland region with Norway and Sweden. It is named for the reindeer-herding Lapp, or Sami, our indigenous people. Inspired by my frozen landscape, Finnish composer Jean Sibelius (1865–1957) claimed his sixth symphony reminded him of the scent of the first snow. Head to my far north and you'll see how the "midnight" sun stays above the horizon from mid-May until July. In winter, the northern lights—splashes of pink, green, violet, and yellow light—flash across my darkened skies. Known as the "aurora borealis," this show is created by solar particles smashing into Earth's atmospheric gases. Sami legend holds that whistling to the lights brings bad luck, lest they swoop down and spirit you away.

I may sound primitive but, trust me, I most definitely am not! My capital Helsinki, known as the Pearl of the Baltic, is home to the textile factory in which the bold and colorful Marimekko fabrics come to life.

● **SIZE:** 130,559 sq mi (338,145 sq km)

● **POPULATION:** 5,498,000

● **CURRENCY:** Euro

● **CAPITAL:** Helsinki

○ **LANGUAGES:** Finnish, Swedish

Republic of Ireland

✳ Ireland became a republic in 1949, when it severed its ties with the United Kingdom

✳ Dublin's O'Connell Bridge over the Liffey River is as wide as it is long

SIZE: 27,133 sq mi (70,273 sq km)

POPULATION: 4,952,000

CURRENCY: Euro

CAPITAL: Dublin

LANGUAGES: English, Gaelic

True, I'm known as the Emerald Isle, but don't get your hopes up. There are no caverns of precious jewels here. (Don't expect to find any leprechauns, either, with their tiny pots of gold!) No, my intense green hue—visible even in satellite images—is due to grass: More than 80 percent of me is covered with the stuff. Whether wild or cultivated, it thrives due to the moderating climate influence of the North Atlantic Current, a branch of the Gulf Stream. Grazing animals stay on my rich pastures for nearly 300 days a year; the intense yellow of Irish butter is due to the cows' natural diet.

Boy does it rain here—as much as 39 inches (100 cm) fall in the east per year and 55 inches (140 cm) in the west. And would you believe that I'm Europe's second-least forested country (after Iceland)? No one knows why exactly, but by the end of the 19th century, the broadleaf forest that once covered me had disappeared. Most likely, my people simply cut it all down for fuel, homes, and ships.

United Kingdom

EUROPE

* The clocktower at London's Westminster Palace is Elizabeth Tower; its bell is "Big Ben"
* In 2016, U.K. citizens voted for "Brexit"—a withdrawal from the European Union
* All horses, donkeys, and ponies living in the U.K. must have a passport

Watch me evolve. I've been tramped across by lots of people: Picts, Celts, Romans, Anglo Saxons . . . Many have left their mark, from Stonehenge in my south to Hadrian's Wall in my north. My government has changed from an absolute monarchy in Tudor times to a constitutional monarchy, with a head of state (my fab queen) and a prime minister heading a democratically elected parliament. I've suffered (the bubonic plague, the Great Fire of London, the Blitz), but I was once head of the largest empire ever known. Today, 14 overseas territories remain within my jurisdiction and I am one of the world's biggest donors of foreign aid.

So what's my secret? (Not my cuisine . . . others sneer at the way I overcook vegetables.) Maybe it's my mild climate? Influenced by the North Atlantic Current, it is perfect for farming—almost 70 percent of my land is agricultural. Or perhaps it's my gentle geography—stunning hill-climbing highlands to the north and rolling lowlands to the south? Some might even say my good fortune is down to my people. I've known charismatic rulers (Elizabeth I, Winston Churchill) and artists to die for (William Shakespeare, The Beatles). What's more, today, my population represents over 60 ethnic groups and every major religion.

- **SIZE:** 94,058 sq mi (243,610 sq km)
- **POPULATION:** 64,430,000
- **CURRENCY:** British pound sterling
- **CAPITAL:** London
- **LANGUAGE:** English

From Mainland to Island

Around 18,000 years ago, the U.K. was attached to the northwestern edge of Europe. Around 6000 B.C.E., three huge landslides beneath the sea created a tsunami that ripped the land from the continent.

Four in One

The United Kingdom is made up of four nations. Besides England, the nations and their respective capitals are: Scotland (Edinburgh), Wales (Cardiff), and Northern Ireland (Belfast). Once governed solely from London, each nation has been legally given certain governing powers in recent years.

Spain

EUROPE

- The spires of Antoni Gaudí's Sagrada Familia dominate the Barcelona skyline
- Andalusia, in the south, is home to a form of song, dance, and music called "flamenco"

I occupy most of the Iberian Peninsula, an ancient name that refers to my Ebro River. After climbing the Pyrenees on my northern border with France or the Sierra Nevada mountains that protect my southern reaches, kick back on the Meseta—the high central plateau that dominates my interior.

If a country were a recipe, I'd be the exotic one with a list of distinct flavors. To my north is the Basque country, where a very proud nation has sought independence from Spain in recent years. Then there are the Catalans. Centered around vibrant Barcelona in my northeast, these guys consider themselves a separate nation already. My Alhambra Palace in Granada was built by the Moors, who arrived from North Africa in the sixth century. Thanks to my climate, I have a wealth of sun-blessed fruits and vegetables to throw into the pot: oranges, mangoes, grapes, tomatoes, and onions. And where the Mediterranean meets the Atlantic, my seas are full of red mullet, tuna, and octopus.

- **SIZE:** 195,124 sq mi (505,370 sq km)
- **POPULATION:** 48,563,000
- **CURRENCY:** Euro
- **CAPITAL:** Madrid
- **LANGUAGE:** Spanish

Portugal
EUROPE

✴ Portugal's largest river, the Tagus, flows west from Spain and is 626 miles (1007 km) long
✴ Glazed ceramic tiles introduced by the Moors decorate many façades and interiors

Sometimes I'm tempted to slip my moorings off the edge of the Iberian Peninsula and sail away into the Atlantic. Who knows what I'd discover? After all, my Prince Henry the Navigator is said to have kickstarted the Age of Discovery with his maritime endeavors of the 1400s. Swashbucklers Vasco da Gama and Ferdinand Magellan soon followed. These men put wind in the sails of Europe's rush toward colonization and gained major riches for me! And what better sight to behold on returning home, than the iconic Belém Tower rising from my Lisbon shores.

With 500 miles (800 km) of coastline along the Atlantic Ocean, not to mention my two archipelagos (take a bow—Madeira and the Azores), it's little wonder I'm so drawn to the sea. Just look at my exports—one-fifth of them are fish, such as sardines and tuna. In fact, I am a fan of water all round: My mountainous north sees as much as five times the rain that falls in my low-lying south.

○ **SIZE:** 35,556 sq mi (92,090 sq km)

● **POPULATION:** 10,834,000

◎ **CURRENCY:** Euro

● **CAPITAL:** Lisbon

○ **LANGUAGE:** Portuguese

Andorra

EUROPE

So, I resemble a cute belly button nestling in the mountainous midriff between Spain and France—don't laugh! I've been around since 1278, when a charter was signed establishing my sovereignty. I'm so mountainous that almost all of my buildings sit in valleys— even the Casa de la Vall, home to my General Council. Mountains have an upside, though—my Grandvalira ski resort is one of the most popular in the Pyrenees.

- ○ **SIZE:** 181 sq mi (468 sq km)
- ● **POPULATION:** 86,000
- ○ **CURRENCY:** Euro
- ● **CAPITAL:** Andorra la Vella
- ○ **LANGUAGE:** Catalan

Monaco

EUROPE

A principality on the French Riviera, I am ruled by the Grimaldi dynasty; they live in the Prince's Palace, a stronghold since 1297. I've got a coastline you can conquer in a jog: 2.5 miles (4 km) and, boy, what a coastline (yachts galore). I'm all about risk: My casino in Monte Carlo attracts some of the world's richest high rollers, and my Grand Prix is run through my cliff-lined streets instead of on a track!

- ○ **SIZE:** 0.8 sq mi (2 sq km)
- ● **POPULATION:** 31,000
- ○ **CURRENCY:** Euro
- ● **CAPITAL:** Monaco
- ○ **LANGUAGE:** French

Liechtenstein

EUROPE

* Of Liechtenstein's five medieval-era castles, three are ruins and one is a museum
* The last of the five castles—Vaduz Castle—is the king's home

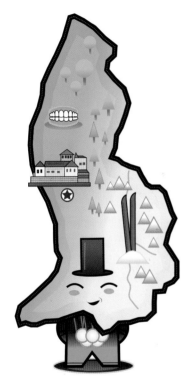

At only 62 square miles (161 sq km), I may be the world's sixth-smallest country, but I offer plenty to sink your teeth into. In fact, check out your grandma's teeth (ask politely)! They were probably made here; I'm the world's largest supplier of dentures.

Wedged in tight between Switzerland and Austria, I get no respect from beach bums: I'm one of only two double-landlocked countries in the world. But another kind of bum—ski bums—love me. You see, about half my land is Alpine mountains. These handsome peaks originated millions of years ago in ancient Africa, would you believe, the result of tremendous tectonic forces beneath Earth's crust. Today, their forests team with wildlife—deer, marmots, hazel grouse, foxes, and stoats. My mountains are heavily regulated to protect against erosion and preserve the ecology of those fine slopes. Oh, and those skiers? They aren't true bums: They've snagged an impressive 11 Olympic medals in Alpine skiing.

- **SIZE:** 62 sq mi (161 sq km)
- **POPULATION:** 38,000
- **CURRENCY:** Swiss franc
- **CAPITAL:** Vaduz
- **LANGUAGE:** German

France

EUROPE

- ☀ The world's first hot-air balloon was created in France by the Montgolfier brothers (1783)
- ☀ The island of Mont St. Michel is joined to France's northeast coast via a bridge
- ☀ Paris is famous for its Eiffel Tower and the cathedral of Notre-Dame

Sacrebleu! I've been through many difficulties to become the *magnifique* country I am today. I've endured invaders, such as Julius Caesar (he took over when I was known as Gaul), and the whims of the Sun King, Louis XIV, with his thing for mirrors (there are 357 of them in just one hall at the Palace of Versailles). I suffered a revolution featuring guillotines, and cruel trench warfare during World War I that took a million and a half of my people's lives.

Still, I have panache (that's style to you): Good bread, cheese, wine, and a perfectly tilted beret help ease the pain. The United Nations awarded my culinary traditions status as a world cultural icon! It's true, I am devoted to products that promote *joie de vivre*: My fertile fields grow the fine things in life, such as grapes for my lovely bubbly champagne. In sunny southern Provence, I grow field after field of fragrant lavender. I cultivate jasmine for the world-famous French perfume, Chanel No. 5. Just one bottle contains 1000 French jasmine buds! Besides my fertile agricultural fields, I am also known for my mountain ranges, of which I have four: the Vosges, Jura, Pyrenees, and, of course, the Alps, site of the first Winter Olympics in the ski resort of Chamonix.

- ○ **SIZE:** 248,573 sq mi (643,801 sq km)
- ● **POPULATION:** 62,814,000
- ◑ **CURRENCY:** Euro
- ● **CAPITAL:** Paris
- ○ **LANGUAGE:** French

Ascend the Podium, *ma Mère!*
The French government awards mothers with many children the Medal of the French Family: Bronze for six children, silver for seven, and if you can go the distance with eight, Mom (*mère*) takes the gold.

Overseas Territories

France's territories include Guadeloupe and Martinique in the Caribbean, French Guiana in South America, and Réunion and Mayotte in the Indian Ocean. Designated "overseas departments," their people have the same rights as those in regions of mainland France.

Netherlands

EUROPE

※ Keukenhof, in the town of Lisse, is home to the world's best-known tulip festival

※ The Dutch women's field hockey team has won the World Cup a record seven times

Go with the flow? No way. Flooding is not my thing. In the contest between the Netherlands and the North Sea, it's advantage Netherlands. In 1953, a storm breached aging dikes and killed 1800 people, so I got serious about flood control. Today, I deploy canals, dikes, artificial dunes planted with grass to create dense, absorbent mats, and enormous floating gates that close when tides surge. Otherwise, I'd be drowned, because almost half my land is below sea level.

My water-wrangling smarts mean that my population prospers. After the U.S., I am the second-largest exporter of agricultural products in the world—flowers, meat, dairy—and grow one-quarter of all the vegetables exported from Europe. Did you know that my Amsterdam airport and Rotterdam seaport are among the world's busiest today? Well, I've had trade in my bones for centuries, peaking with the establishment of the Dutch East India Company in the 1600s.

○ **SIZE:** 16,040 sq mi (41,543 sq km)

○ **POPULATION:** 17,017,000

○ **CURRENCY:** Euro

● **CAPITAL:** Amsterdam

○ **LANGUAGE:** Dutch

Belgium

EUROPE

Aconvenient rendezvous point for some of the bloodiest battles of two world wars, is it any wonder I've made diplomacy my business? My capital, Brussels, is home to the headquarters of NATO and the EU. My people get testy at times, with deep divisions between my southern Walloons and my northern Flemings. But my most serious debate is with France, and whether or not French fries are, in fact, Belgian. They are!

- **SIZE:** 11,787 sq mi (30,528 sq km)
- **POPULATION:** 11,409,000
- **CURRENCY:** Euro
- **CAPITAL:** Brussels
- **LANGUAGES:** Dutch, French, German

Luxembourg

EUROPE

I originated as a fortress and castle built on a strategic promontory known as the Bock, which stands inside a loop of the Alzette River. Views from the top look out over my lush Bon Pays region. I grew outward from the castle, while the castle grew deep into the ground; over 11 miles (17.5 km) of tunnels remain today! In World War II, General George Patton liberated me from German occupation in the Battle of the Bulge, and today I am his burial ground.

- **SIZE:** 998 sq mi (2586 sq km)
- **POPULATION:** 582,000
- **CURRENCY:** Euro
- **CAPITAL:** Luxembourg City
- **LANGUAGES:** Luxembourgish, French, German

Switzerland

EUROPE

- Switzerland is famous for chocolate, cheese, luxury watches, and ski resorts
- At 331 feet (101 m) high, Bern's cathedral spire is the tallest in Switzerland

- **SIZE:** 15,937 sq mi (41,277 sq km)
- **POPULATION:** 8,179,000
- **CURRENCY:** Euro
- **CAPITAL:** Bern
- **LANGUAGES:** German, French, Italian, Romansch

Landlocked, I have a landscape dominated by the Swiss Alps and the Jura Mountains. My Alps are home to the Cresta Run skeleton bobsled track at St. Moritz and Europe's highest train station, 13,642 feet (4158 m), up at Jungfrau peak. Between the mountain ranges, my Swiss plateau is home to two major cities, Geneva and Zurich. And I still have room for more than 1500 lakes—Geneva and Constance are two of Europe's largest.

I'm neutral, but that doesn't mean I'm boring. You see, after the Napoleonic Wars (when I was invaded by France, in 1798), my European neighbors saw my potential as a military buffer zone. In 1815, I was declared "perpetually neutral." I am also proud of the moment that Swiss John-Henri Dunant founded the Red Cross, an organization that protects victims of conflict. His idea won him the first Nobel Peace Prize, in 1901.

Austria

EUROPE

- ❋ The Austrian city of Innsbruck has hosted the Winter Olympics twice
- ❋ The Danube, Europe's second-longest river, crosses Austria from east to west

- ● **SIZE:** 32,383 sq mi (83,871 sq km)
- ● **POPULATION:** 8,712,000
- ● **CURRENCY:** Euro
- ● **CAPITAL:** Vienna
- ● **LANGUAGE:** German

Shall we dance? The Viennese Waltz, of course! My waltz is just one of the traditions I'm famed for, as are competitive cowbell ringing and yodeling—important skills if you're a cowherd trying to call in the cows or communicate with a pal living across the valley. You see, about two-thirds of my land is Alpine mountains, and one-third of my people live in the valleys. In the olden days before texting, yodeling was a great way

to make a date to meet for Wiener Schnitzel (my traditional dish, a breaded veal cutlet).

Still, I'm so much more than yodeling cow herders. The Staatsoper (State Opera House) in Vienna is fabled for its elaborate shows. And if you love pastry, you might never want to leave; my coffee houses offer the richest *tortes* around, such as my jam-filled Linzer Torte, the world's oldest cake.

Italy

EUROPE

* Landmarks include Brunelleschi's Dome in Florence and Rome's Colosseum
* The "ball" that Italy's "boot" is kicking is the island of Sicily

I'm one country that's hard to contain. If my innards aren't rumbling (I sit on a fault line between the African and Eurasian tectonic plates, so I'm highly prone to earthquakes), they're spewing—I'm home to Europe's three active volcanoes: Etna, Stromboli, and Vesuvius. And don't hate me for being beautiful! I may be shaped like an old boot, but there is nothing inelegant or down-at-heel about me. I'm overflowing with art, such as Michelangelo's statue of David and Canaletto's paintings of Venetian canals (gondolas, and all). My ancient monuments, the Roman Forum and the Trevi Fountain, are fabled for their beauty, but don't forget my earthier marvels of the past: The Cloaca Maxima, or great sewer, dates from 6 B.C.E. and channels Roman wastewater to this day.

It may also give you a jolt to know that I can claim Alessandro Volta as a native son. He was the scientist who invented the first battery by analysing twitching frog legs. (It's a galvanizing story.)

○ **SIZE:** 116,348 sq mi (301,340 sq km)

○ **POPULATION:** 62,008,000

○ **CURRENCY:** Euro

● **CAPITAL:** Rome

○ **LANGUAGE:** Italian

San Marino

EUROPE

Buried inside Italy, I've been sitting pretty atop Mount Titano in the Apennine Mountains since 301 C.E., when Marinus, a Croatian stonecutter, founded a monastery. I'm one of the world's oldest states! Today, you can visit my three medieval fortresses with superb Adriatic vistas and contemplate the artifacts in my Museum of Torture. You'll need a strong stomach; they have a knee-breaker, a traction bench, and an iron maiden.

- ○ **SIZE:** 24 sq mi (61 sq km)
- ○ **POPULATION:** 33,000
- ○ **CURRENCY:** Euro
- ● **CAPITAL:** City of San Marino
- ○ **LANGUAGE:** Italian

Vatican City

EUROPE

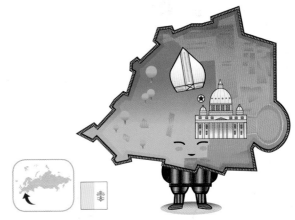

Holier than thou? You bet I am! A walled enclave in Rome, I'm divinely tiny, the world's smallest sovereign state. I boast some highly connected residents (the Pope, not to name drop). St. Peter's Basilica, where the Pope celebrates mass, is built over the tombs of medieval popes and the apostle Peter. And while my Swiss Guards may look harmless in their striped pantaloons, don't cross them; they are expert marksmen!

- ○ **SIZE:** 0.17 sq mi (0.44 sq km)
- ○ **POPULATION:** 1000
- ○ **CURRENCY:** Euro
- ● **CAPITAL:** Vatican City
- ○ **LANGUAGE:** Italian

Germany

EUROPE

- Berlin's Zoologischer Garten is the world's largest zoo: 84 acres (0.34 sq km)
- The Brandenburg Gate, in Berlin, is the site of many historical events
- Skyscraper-filled Frankfurt is home to the European Central Bank

Don't be afraid—come in under the dark evergreen canopy of my Schwarzwald, or Black Forest. It's nothing sinister—black just refers to the dark shadows created by the conifers. On second thoughts, perhaps you should be cautious. After all, my Brothers Grimm (again, don't let the name spook you) are world-famous for their folk stories of child-eating witches living in tempting candy cottages and ravenous wolves nestled deep in Grandma's feather bed. And if fairy tales are your thing, don't forget to pass by Lorelei, the murmuring rock in the middle of my Rhine River, where a fabled golden-haired siren has caused many a shipwreck.

If, as you journey through my land, you think you hear music, it could be the ghosts of my composers, who practically invented classical music: Bach, Beethoven, Brahms . . . I could go on. Their chords reach to the rafters of my imposing cathedrals, such as Cologne (it took 632 years to build and can hold 40,000 people) or Freiburg, with its 44-stop organ that Mozart himself praised. Life in modern Germany is prosperous: My export economy is the world's largest—bigger even than China's. As in many developed countries, though, the population is declining, and from 1989 to 2009, 2000 German schools were closed because there were not enough children!

- **SIZE:** 137,847 sq mi (357,022 sq km)
- **POPULATION:** 80,723,000
- **CURRENCY:** Euro
- **CAPITAL:** Berlin
- **LANGUAGE:** German

Prize Pickles

The gherkins of Germany's Spreewald region are so crunchy and spicy that they are protected by the European Union. They boast their own cuke-friendly bicycle route known in English as the Pickle Path.

Shifting Borders

Before Germany became a nation-state, in 1871, the region had been a collection of small, mostly German-speaking states. In 1949, following World War II, the country was divided once more—into East and West (even Berlin was divided by the Berlin Wall). The two halves were reunited in 1990.

Poland

EUROPE

☀ Polish Marie Curie was the first woman to win a Nobel Prize (for discovering radium)

☀ *Pysanky*, or decorated Easter eggs, are a traditional Polish craft

- **SIZE:** 1186 sq mi (3071 sq km)
- **POPULATION:** 38,523,000
- **CURRENCY:** Polish zloty
- **CAPITAL:** Warsaw
- **LANGUAGE:** Polish

You would need time-lapse photography to keep track of my shifting borders over the years. In 1492, I was the largest territory in Europe, but by 1795, Russia, Prussia, and Austria had all but gobbled me up. I didn't exist again as a country until the end of World War I.

Oh, but what a fine country, with supertall Tatras Mountains on my border with Slovakia and the stunning Masurian Lake District in my northeastern corner. My longest river, the Vistula, winds its way from north to south, cutting me in half. My Palace of Culture and Science in Warsaw is the eighth-tallest building in Europe, while Gdańsk is one of the busiest ports on the Baltic Sea. My Wieliczka Salt Mine near Krakow has existed since the 13th century and boasts an underground salt cathedral and three chandeliers of crystallized rock salt.

Estonia

EUROPE

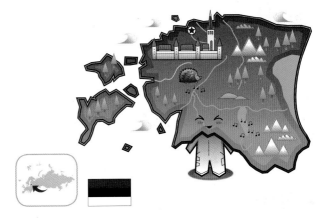

Located between the Baltic Sea and the Gulf of Finland, I'm a flat, forested land of equal parts tradition and innovation. While the warrior hero of my national epic poem, *Kalevipoeg*, took battle advice from a hedgehog, more recently my people helped invent Skype. Chorale singing is a favorite pastime, a way to establish unity and express national pride as we twice (in 1918 and 1991) fought for independence from the Soviet Union.

- **SIZE:** 17,463 sq mi (45,228 sq km)
- **POPULATION:** 1,259,000
- **CURRENCY:** Euro
- **CAPITAL:** Tallinn
- **LANGUAGE:** Estonian

Latvia

EUROPE

Situated on the northern Baltic Sea, but with ice-free ports, I'm a land of forests, bogs, 12,000 rivers, and 3000 little lakes. I'm good for what ails you! I offer remedies from the woods: My national liqueur is brewed from 24 plants, buds, juices, roots, plant oils, and berries. Following occupations by Germany, Poland, Sweden, and the Soviet Union, events that led to my independence in 1991 are known as the Singing Revolution.

- **SIZE:** 24,938 sq mi (64,589 sq km)
- **POPULATION:** 1,966,000
- **CURRENCY:** Euro
- **CAPITAL:** Riga
- **LANGUAGES:** Latvian, Russian

Lithuania

EUROPE

Exposed on the Baltic Sea, I've been invaded by Russia, Sweden, and Germany among others. No wonder, then, that my national symbol is Vytis, a white knight mounted on a rearing stallion, brandishing his broadsword. Having gained independence from the Soviet Union in 1991, I still have many Soviet-era buildings—apartment blocks and a super-skinny TV tower. But my capital also has one of Europe's largest old-town districts.

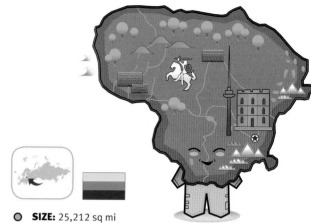

- **SIZE:** 25,212 sq mi (65,300 sq km)
- **POPULATION:** 2,854,000
- **CURRENCY:** Euro
- **CAPITAL:** Vilnius
- **LANGUAGE:** Lithuanian

Slovakia

EUROPE

I split from the Czechs in 1993 and I'm so proud! The name of my capital, Bratislava, is just a big brag: It combines root words for "brotherhood" and "glory." My High Tatras Mountains are the tallest in central Europe and offer killer ski resorts. I'm also cave central. My karst (eroded limestone) region has 712 caves—sometimes used for aging wine. The Dobsinská Ice Cave is superchilled: Its temperature never rises above zero.

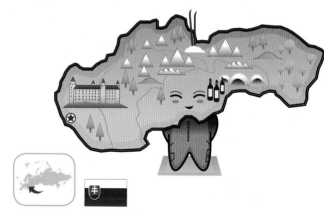

- **SIZE:** 18,933 sq mi (49,035 sq km)
- **POPULATION:** 5,446,000
- **CURRENCY:** Euro
- **CAPITAL:** Bratislava
- **LANGUAGE:** Slovak

Czech Republic

※ ● The Czech Republic has more than 2000 castles, castle ruins, and keeps
※ ● Prague's 15th-century Charles Bridge has more than 30 statues of Christian saints

○ **SIZE:** 30,451 sq mi
(78,867 sq km)
◉ **POPULATION:**
10,645,000
○ **CURRENCY:**
Czech koruna
● **CAPITAL:**
Prague
○ **LANGUAGE:**
Czech

A landlocked middleman, I have three main regions, Bohemia, Moravia, and Silesia. My people are watched over by St. Vitus, who is said to protect against lightning, dog bites, and oversleeping. My approachable terrain—gently rolling hills and low forested mountains—means that, for centuries, I've been a friendly travel route for traders, funneling them along the Amber Road, an ancient trade route between the Baltic and Mediterranean Seas. My Vltava River slices my capital in two as it journeys 270 miles (435 km) across my land.

Recent history? Well, Slovakia and I were once a single country (Czechoslovakia) under Communist control. In 1989, our people staged a revolution to set us free. Then Slovakia and I decided to go our separate ways in 1993. Today, I like to call myself Czechia for short.

Hungary

EUROPE

* Budapest's parliament building sits on the banks of the Danube River
* Relaxing in Budapest's thermal baths is a way of life for some

- **SIZE:** 35,918 sq mi (93,028 sq km)
- **POPULATION:** 9,875,000
- **CURRENCY:** Hungarian forint
- **CAPITAL:** Budapest
- **LANGUAGE:** Hungarian

Flat to rolling plains are the hallmark of my land, divided by the Danube River flowing north to south on its way to the Black Sea. And no, I'm not *hungry*, thank you. We eat well here—ever heard of Hungarian goulash? The Hungarian word for it, *gulyásleves*, means "herdsmen's soup"—cooked by the cowboys!

Hungaria was a medieval name for me, but I also call my people Magyars, for the warrior tribe that roamed me in the ninth century. Love those guys—led by their Grand Prince, Arpád, they migrated across the Carpathian Mountains to conquer and settle my land.

I was worth grabbing; I'm home to Europe's largest thermal lake, Hévíz. Situated on an ancient peat bed, its waters are said to be medicinal! I also boast Europe's largest natural grasslands—the Puszta.

Romania

EUROPE

* Romania's Statue of Decebalus, in Orsova, is Europe's largest rock sculpture
* Timisoara was the first European city to have electric street lights (1884)

I boast a stretch of Black Sea coastline fed by the great Danube River. My Danube Delta, Europe's second-longest river delta, is made up of an intricate network of marshes, lagoons, and streamlets. They provide secluded habitats for endangered birds, such as the Dalmatian pelican and great cormorant. But let's face it: People know me best for my forbidding Carpathian Mountains, home to Europe's highest concentration of brown bears, wolves, and lynxes. The range cuts a path across me from north to southwest. And don't forget my castles—I have at least ten—or the Palace of Parliament in my capital, Bucharest. It happens to be the world's second-largest administrative building after the Pentagon in Washington, D.C.

Back to my castles, though, and the ruin of Poenari Castle, in particular. Looming in grim isolation on one of my Carpathian peaks, it's one of the many rumored haunts of Vlad the Impaler. Yes, Count Dracula—my favorite son!

○ **SIZE:** 92,043 sq mi (238,391 sq km)

◉ **POPULATION:** 21,600,000

○ **CURRENCY:** Romanian leu

◉ **CAPITAL:** Bucharest

○ **LANGUAGE:** Romanian

Serbia

EUROPE

- ☀ Serbia's capital, Belgrade, sits at the point at which the Danube and Sava rivers meet
- ☀ Wolves roam the Deliblato Sands desert to the north of the country

Take my word for it: I'm tough. I need to be—the Balkan peninsula, my home, has been ravaged by conflict for centuries, as my neighbors and I have fought for our independence. First we battled against the Ottoman Empire and then against each other! My rugged topography matches my reputation: The Dinaric Alps slash through my southwest; to the east, the Balkan Mountains warn off Romania and Bulgaria. At least my climate isn't fearsome: Continental in the north and Adriatic in the south, it's ideal for growing fruit. I export tons of delicious raspberries, plums, and apples.

Culturally, I am buzzing with a wealth of national crafts and traditions: Kilim-rug weaving thrives in my southeastern city of Pirot, while Kovačica, in the Vojvodina region to my north, is a center for a "naïve" style of folk-art painting. My lively country dances include the *kolo*, in which people clasp arms to dance in a circle, and the *lesa*, which involves two parallel lines of linked dancers.

- ● **SIZE:** 29,913 sq. mi. (77,474 sq km)
- ● **POPULATION:** 7,144,000
- ● **CURRENCY:** Serbian dinar
- ● **CAPITAL:** Belgrade
- ● **LANGUAGE:** Serbian

Slovenia

EUROPE

Alpine mountains dominate my north, while caves and underground rivers riddle my south. Head east and you'll find fertile land, good for growing wheat. It's miniature, but I even boast a coastline on the Adriatic Sea. My heritage is Slavic, but I'm geographically close to Italy: Venice lies just across the water. I have a passion for the art of puppetry and Ljubljana, my capital, hosts a famed Puppet Theater and Museum.

- **SIZE:** 7827 sq mi (20,273 sq km)
- **POPULATION:** 1,978,000
- **CURRENCY:** Euro
- **CAPITAL:** Ljubljana
- **LANGUAGE:** Slovene

Montenegro

EUROPE

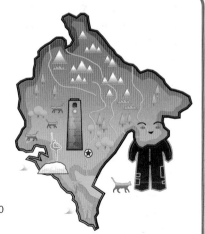

I stuck with Serbia when the rest of Yugoslavia went bye-bye in 2003. But in 2006, I voted to go my own way. Check out my mountain gorges, monasteries, and mausoleums—what's not to like? Don't pet my feral cats. My medieval city Kotor, is kitty central! Its Cats Museum features a complete cluster of catty exhibits. And on my Mogren Beach near Budva, a statue of a woman confronts the waves in an awesome ballet pose!

- **SIZE:** 5333 sq mi (13,812 sq km)
- **POPULATION:** 645,000
- **CURRENCY:** Euro
- **CAPITAL:** Podgorica
- **LANGUAGES:** Serbian, Montenegrin

Croatia

EUROPE

※ An equestrian statue of military hero Josip Jelacic stands in a square in the capital

※ The spotted Dalmatian dog originated in the Dalmatia region of Croatia

Just across the Adriatic Sea from Italy, I'm shaped like an irregular pair of tweezers with a 1120-mile (1800-km) coastline and the handle of the Istrian peninsula jutting into the sea to my north. My rural fields are dotted with *kazun*—stone shelters with conical roofs that were used for storage and shelter for olive-grove workers during the days of the Roman Empire.

At my southern tip, thick stone walls that date from the ninth century encircle my ancient city of Dubrovnik, and are topped with forts. And how many modern city centers get built in the middle of a palace? Split, on my Istrian peninsula, is just that: Hip restaurants, shops, and homes sit within and around the Emperor Diocletian's Palace, dating from 295 C.E. Some of the white limestone used to construct that palace came from my island of Brac. The White House in Washington, D.C. is built with the same glittering white stone. Little wonder I'm known as the pearl of the Adriatic!

○ **SIZE:** 21,851 sq mi (56,594 sq km)

◉ **POPULATION:** 4,314,000

○ **CURRENCY:** Croatian kuna

● **CAPITAL:** Zagreb

○ **LANGUAGE:** Croatian

Bosnia & Herzegovina

EUROPE

✳ The capital, Sarajevo, was the first European city to have an electric tram
✳ Sarajevo's modern skyline is pierced by the Avaz Twist Tower, with a twisted façade

- ○ **SIZE:** 19,767 sq mi (51,197 sq km)
- ◉ **POPULATION:** 3,862,000
- ○ **CURRENCY:** Bosnian convertible marka
- ● **CAPITAL:** Sarajevo
- ○ **LANGUAGES:** Bosnian, Serbian, Croatian

My double name links the names of my two regions: northern Bosnia and southern Herzegovina. My landscape is dominated by the Dinaric Alps, primeval forests, and many rivers, including the Neretva in Mostar, famed for its emerald color. My karst plateau near Montenegro in the south features a limestone terrain riddled with caves and potholes. At least seven waterfalls scattered in my mountains boast multiple cascades. Splash!

I'm also rich in mineral ores; horseshoes were once an export and my traditional handicrafts include engraved metalwork.

Ottoman ruler Suleiman the Magnificent ordered the building of the iconic Starí Most Bridge in the city of Mostar, during the 16th century. Destroyed by shelling in the Croat-Bosniak War (1992–1994), its reincarnation uses some of the original pale stone.

Macedonia

EUROPE

I'm a landlocked region of mountains and lakes on the northern border of Greece. Poor but proud, I have recently splashed out on a new dome for my parliament. My Lake Ohrid is one of the world's oldest and deepest. It's a squishy-stuff museum, with snails and sponges found nowhere else on Earth. And I must be doing something right: I'm the only former Yugoslav republic to achieve independence without bloodshed.

- **SIZE:** 9928 sq mi (25,713 sq km)
- **POPULATION:** 2,100,000
- **CURRENCY:** Macedonian denar
- **CAPITAL:** Skopje
- **LANGUAGE:** Macedonian

Albania

EUROPE

A small mountainous country, my long Adriatic coastline sports untouristy beaches. Inland, my lush fertile plains provide top spots for agriculture. I'm not a rich country; perhaps that inspired my revered native saint, Mother Teresa. Dotted around my landscape are 750,000 concrete bunkers—a legacy from my Communist past—now painted in bright colors and used as shelters for the homeless and as food kiosks!

- **SIZE:** 11,100 sq mi (28,748 sq km)
- **POPULATION:** 3,039,000
- **CURRENCY:** Albanian lek
- **CAPITAL:** Tirana
- **LANGUAGE:** Albanian

Bulgaria
EUROPE

- ✳ Bulgaria's Rose Valley is the world's largest producer of rose oil for perfume
- ✳ Thick sheep's yogurt made in the mountains is some of the best in the world

- ○ **SIZE:** 42, 811 sq mi (110,879 sq km)
- ◉ **POPULATION:** 7,145,000
- ○ **CURRENCY:** Bulgarian lev
- ● **CAPITAL:** Sofia
- ○ **LANGUAGE:** Bulgarian

Founded in the seventh century, I'm one of Europe's oldest states. My people were Bulgars—seminomadic, equestrian warriors.

In my more recent history, I sided with the Axis powers (Germany, Italy, and Japan) during World War II. Later, in the 1990s, I managed to shake off Soviet domination, and now I take pride in being a member of NATO and the EU.

A northern Danubian plain rolls inland from my coast on the Black Sea. In my southwest, you'll find the Rila and Rhodope mountains. Something super-healthy must be happening in those peaks and valleys because the region is home to the world's highest percentage of centenarians (people 100 years old, and over). My Kukeri festival sees dancers wearing furry hooded costumes cavorting through villages at dawn to ward off evil spirits.

Greece

EUROPE

* The Parthenon, a temple in Athens, honors the Greek goddess, Athena
* The island of Santorini is a caldera, the result of a volcanic eruption

Surrounded by four seas—the Aegean, Ionian, Cretan, and Mediterranean—is it any wonder I count Odysseus, the adventurer who set sail from my Ionian isle, Ithaca, among my heroes? You'll find me at the tip of the Balkan peninsula plus a clutch of tiny islands (around 6000—who's counting, only 227 are inhabited). Some call me the cradle of Western civilization. Sure, I'll take a bow.

I'm 80 percent mountainous. You may have heard of my highest peak, Mount Olympus, where that old god Zeus lives. Don't confuse it with Olympia, though, site of the original Olympic Games—the two are hundreds of miles apart. My largest island, Crete, marks the southernmost limit of Europe. It served as the epicenter of Minoan civilization and dates back to 3000 B.C.E. Perhaps you think I make too much of my history, but all of my greatest assets have been around since that time. Honey, olive oil, wine, and figs—all of them ancient and now major exports, along with natural sea sponges and Greek marble.

- **SIZE:** 50,948 sq mi (131,957 sq km)
- **POPULATION:** 10,773,000
- **CURRENCY:** Euro
- **CAPITAL:** Athens
- **LANGUAGE:** Greek

Cyprus

EUROPE

A beautiful island in the Mediterranean Sea, I'm cut in two by a UN-patrolled buffer zone. You see, my Turkish Cypriots have laid claim to my north from the rest of my Greek-dominated island. I'm skimmed by two mountain ranges north and south of a central plain. Near my city of Paphos, lie ancient ruins honoring Aphrodite, the Greek goddess of love. According to legend, she first touched land on my shore after rising from the sea on a scallop shell.

- **SIZE:** 3572 sq mi (9251 sq km)
- **POPULATION:** 1,206,000
- **CURRENCY:** Euro
- **CAPITAL:** Nicosia
- **LANGUAGES:** Greek, Turkish

Malta

EUROPE

I was once connected to the ancient African supercontinent; scientists have unearthed elephant fossils in my caves! Now I'm a Mediterranean island archipelago. Steep limestone cliffs with pretty coves and bays dominate my coastlines. In 1530, Emperor Charles V granted my sovereignty to the crusader Knights of St. John. Since then, I've been French and British, but I like being independent best of all!

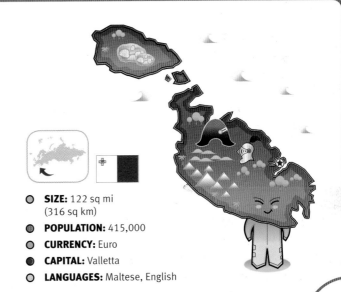

- **SIZE:** 122 sq mi (316 sq km)
- **POPULATION:** 415,000
- **CURRENCY:** Euro
- **CAPITAL:** Valletta
- **LANGUAGES:** Maltese, English

Belarus

EUROPE

Landlocked, I consist mostly of lowlands with some stylish, flat-topped hills in my northwest—the Belarusian Ridge. In Vitebsk to the northeast, *zubr*, (that's European bison to you) roam the Berezinsky Biosphere Reserve. They are the continent's largest living mammal. If you think my capital's Gorky Park, established in 1800, seems old, think again. My Bialowieza Forest is primeval— from the earliest time in history.

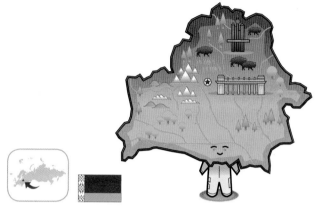

- **SIZE:** 80,155 sq mi (207,600 sq km)
- **POPULATION:** 9,570,000
- **CURRENCY:** Belarusian ruble
- **CAPITAL:** Minsk
- **LANGUAGES:** Russian, Belarusian

Moldova

EUROPE

Tiny but spirited, I have rolling plains and superrich soils; both are ideal for growing crops for export—grains and beet in the north and grapes in the south. My Milestii Mici wine cellar rates as super cool. Created from an old limestone mine, its 124 miles (200 km) of tunnels can be navigated by car or bus! Step into the forests that grow in my Dniester River floodplain and you might just spot a white-tailed sea eagle.

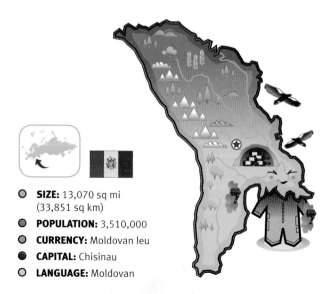

- **SIZE:** 13,070 sq mi (33,851 sq km)
- **POPULATION:** 3,510,000
- **CURRENCY:** Moldovan leu
- **CAPITAL:** Chisinau
- **LANGUAGE:** Moldovan

Ukraine

EUROPE

* Ukraine is one of Europe's largest grain exporters, a crucial breadbasket
* The world's worst nuclear energy accident occurred at Chernobyl, in Ukraine, in 1986

- **SIZE:** 233,032 sq mi (603,550 sq km)
- **POPULATION:** 44,210,000
- **CURRENCY:** Ukrainian hryvnia
- **CAPITAL:** Kiev
- **LANGUAGE:** Ukrainian

Situated north of the Black Sea in eastern Europe, I've been a prized land for many centuries and remain so—in recent years, Russia annexed my Crimean peninsula.

The Dnieper River, an ancient trade route on the Amber Road, flows through Kiev, my capital. In the 17th and 18th centuries, my people were Cossacks, daring horsemen and warriors of the steppes. These days, crops take up swathes of those Cossack lands; their rich, black soil is notoriously fertile. I'm big on seeds for oils—sunflower, hemp, poppy—and beets. Potatoes (I am one of Europe's largest exporters) grow farther north. Check out the primeval beech forests of my Carpathian Mountains or the ancient city of Chersonesus on the shores of the Black Sea—just two of my seven (that's right, seven) UNESCO World Heritage sites.

Russia

EUROPE

* The world's largest country by surface area—almost twice the size of the United States
* The Trans-Siberian Railway runs for 5778 miles (9298 km) from Moscow to Vladivostok
* The Hermitage Museum in St. Petersburg keeps around 70 cats on the lookout for rats

Modesty just isn't me, so I'll say it. I am *epic*. My vast land borders 14 other countries as well as the Arctic and Pacific Oceans, and I have oodles of amazements to boast about. For starters, temperatures in my Siberian tundra can dip as low as −58°F (−50°C). My taiga in the Caucasus region is the world's largest forest and my Mount Elbrus, another Caucasian marvel, is Europe's highest mountain (not to brag, but it's also a volcano). If you're thirsty, there are plenty of refreshing sips in Lake Baikal, the world's oldest (25 million years) and largest freshwater lake. In 1957, my scientists launched *Sputnik I*, Earth's first artificial satellite.

Ever seen a Matryoshka doll? These nesting figures, or "little matrons," were designed by the artist Sergey Malyutin in 1890, and are now popular all over the world. I'm also known for treasures of a more mineral kind. My Mirny Diamond Pit is one of the largest diamond mines in the world. Dig hard enough and you'll find gold, too.

For urban delights, head to Moscow, where the fancy, multicolored onion domes of Saint Basil's Cathedral steal the show in Red Square. Or take in a show at the Bolshoi Ballet, scene of the *grand jeté* and the *demi-plié* for more than 200 years.

○ **SIZE:** 6,601,668 sq mi (17,098,242 sq km)

● **POPULATION:** 142,355,000

◉ **CURRENCY:** Russian ruble

● **CAPITAL:** Moscow

○ **LANGUAGE:** Russian

The Soviet Union

From 1922 until 1991, Russia was the largest and most powerful of 15 states that belonged to the Union of Soviet Socialist Republics. Moscow served as the union's capital and center of government.

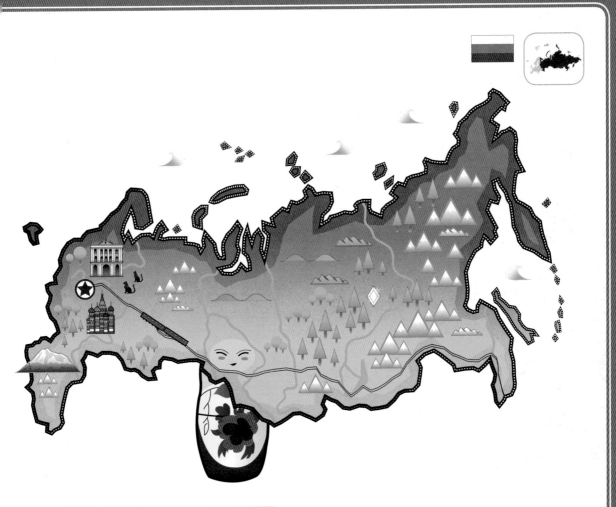

Two Continents

Russia is so vast that it spreads across two continents—Europe and Asia—spanning eleven time zones. The Asian region is by far the largest, yet the majority of Russia's population lives in Europe.

Africa

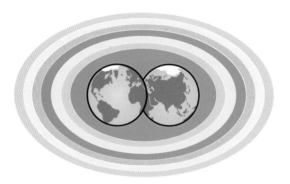

Are your senses up to a trial of strength? Just try to take me in. My Sahara, the world's hottest desert, is as big as the United States. My Serengeti savanna is full of pattern—see the rippling stripes of zebras as they canter across the plain, or the mosaic patches of an elegant giraffe's neck as it reaches to nibble from acacia treetops. In my Kalahari Desert, if you spot a crouched figure aiming a poison-tipped dart, it could be one of Namibia's Ju-Wasi bushmen. Possessors of some of the oldest *Homo sapiens* DNA, these people still live as hunter-gatherers well into the 21st century. How sharp is your ear? You may hear the rippling waters of my Nile, the world's longest river, stocked with grunting hippos and crocodiles, or the distant hum of great cities, such as Nairobi and Johannesburg.

☀ **Land mass:** 11,668,599 sq mi (30,221,532 sq km)

☀ **Number of countries:** 54

☀ **Biggest lake:** Victoria

☀ **Longest river:** Nile

☀ **Highest mountain:** Kilimanjaro

Africa

 Algeria

 Angola

 Benin

 Botswana

 Burkina Faso

 Burundi

 Cameroon

 Cape Verde

 Central African Republic

 Chad

 Comoros

 Congo

 Congo, Democratic Republic of

 Djibouti

 Egypt

 Equatorial Guinea

 Eritrea

 Ethiopia

 Gabon

 Gambia, The

 Ghana

 Guinea

 Guinea-Bissau

 Ivory Coast

 Kenya

 Lesotho

 Liberia

 Libya

 Madagascar

 Malawi

 Mali

 Mauritania

 Mauritius

 Morocco

 Mozambique

 Namibia

 Niger

 Nigeria

 Rwanda

 São Tomé & Príncipe

 Senegal

 Seychelles

 Sierra Leone

 Somalia

 South Africa

 South Sudan

 Sudan

 Swaziland

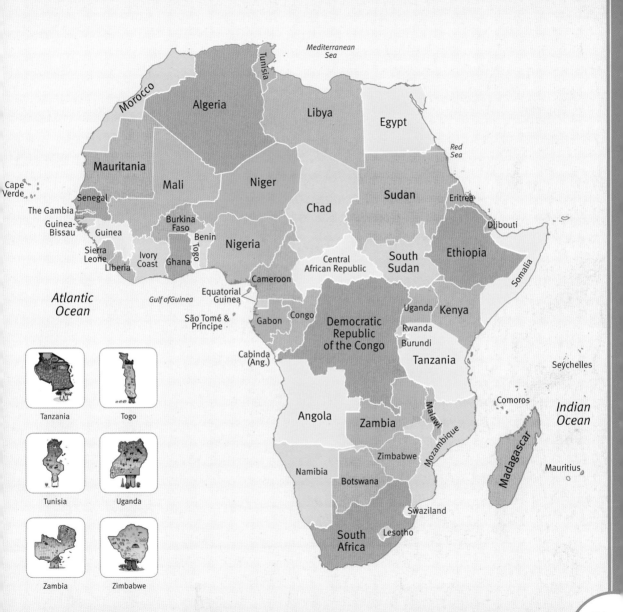

Mediterranean
Sea

Tunisia

Morocco

Algeria

Libya

Egypt

Red
Sea

Mauritania

Mali

Niger

Sudan

Eritrea

Cape
Verde

Senegal

Chad

Djibouti

The Gambia

Guinea-
Bissau

Guinea

Burkina
Faso

Benin

Togo

Nigeria

Central
African Republic

South
Sudan

Ethiopia

Sierra
Leone

Liberia

Ivory
Coast

Ghana

Cameroon

Somalia

Atlantic
Ocean

Gulf of Guinea

Equatorial
Guinea

São Tomé &
Príncipe

Gabon

Congo

Democratic
Republic
of the Congo

Uganda

Rwanda

Burundi

Kenya

Tanzania

Cabinda
(Ang.)

Seychelles

Comoros

Indian
Ocean

Angola

Zambia

Malawi

Mozambique

Madagascar

Mauritius

Zimbabwe

Namibia

Botswana

Swaziland

South
Africa

Lesotho

Tanzania

Togo

Tunisia

Uganda

Zambia

Zimbabwe

91

Morocco

AFRICA

* Chefchaouen village is painted in shades of blue to mirror Morocco's cloudless sky
* Morocco annexed Western Sahara, a territory to the south, in the 1970s

A dual-aspect coastline, the scorching Sahara desert, and two mega mountain ranges—that's me in a nutshell. The Rif mountains border the Mediterranean to my north, while the Atlas Mountains cross me diagonally, northeast to southwest. My indigenous people, the Berbers, live in this rugged terrain. Their ancestors built ancient Marrakesh—a desert city fringed by palms and backed by towering snowy peaks.

In the Atlas foothills, the sweet scents of Persian roses and orange blossoms grown for the perfume trade linger in the air. Talking of scent, the richly ornamented, 14th-century Al-Attarine Madrasa (School of the Perfumers) fronts the perfume market in my medieval city of Fez. You'll see my signature decorative art there—mosaic tiling, or *zellige*. Throughout my land, *zellige* decorates the shady interior courtyard gardens that serve as the peaceful, private hearts of my traditional *riads*, or homes. There's no better place to enjoy my national drink—a glass of sweetened mint tea.

* **SIZE:** 172,414 sq mi (446,550 sq km)
* **POPULATION:** 33,656,000
* **CURRENCY:** Moroccan dirham
* **CAPITAL:** Rabat
* **LANGUAGES:** Arabic, Berber

Algeria

AFRICA

* Algeria is situated in western North Africa, a region that was once called the Maghreb
* Algiers' *casbah* (citadel) once had 150 tiled public water fountains; six remain today

You'll need shades here: I'm famed for the intensity of my light and whitewashed, tumbledown buildings. Dusty desert siroccos blow west across me out to the Mediterranean, and the secluded little ports along my coast were for centuries the favorite haunts of Barbary pirates. In 1575, they captured Miguel de Cervantes, author of *Don Quixote*, and imprisoned him for five years.

The Atlas Mountains dominate my north and the Hoggar Mountains feature in my south, but most of my land is occupied by the scorching Sahara desert. The teensy fennec fox—the world's smallest—lives there and has huge, batlike ears that radiate heat. My coastal capital's *casbah* comprises a steeply pitched hilltop *medina* (village), a *souk* (marketplace), and densely packed houses that have existed since medieval times. The steepest street in the *casbah* has 472 steps. Also on the coast, my city Tipaza contains the ruins of a Roman military outpost with baths, a library, a latrine, and a triumphal arch.

○ **SIZE:** 919,595 sq mi (2,381,741 sq km)

◉ **POPULATION:** 40,264,000

○ **CURRENCY:** Algerian dinar

● **CAPITAL:** Algiers

○ **LANGUAGES:** Arabic, French, Berber

Tunisia

AFRICA

* Tunisian plants include date palms and olive, citrus, cork, and eucalyptus trees
* El Djem's colossal Roman era amphitheater (built 238 c.e.) could hold 35,000 spectators

Gaze out to the Mediterranean from my north African coast, and you can see the Italian island of Sicily on a clear day. My people have worked out exactly how to farm my land: They grow vegetables in my wetter northern region, olives in my central Sahel plain, and dates in my southern Sahara desert. Hot? Just burrow! In Matmata, my cool, earth-sheltered dwellings are tunneled into artificial craters—one even served as Luke Skywalker's home on the planet Tatooine. Or do a breezy island hop: Djerba, connected to my mainland by a Roman-era causeway, is said to be the island of forgetful lotus eaters in Homer's epic poem *The Odyssey*.

Care to shop in the *souk*? Imagine jute sacks of red harissa spice, saffron, and cinnamon; couscous in ancient canisters; brass lanterns; and piles of oriental carpets. But how to get around? Never mind used-car lots: I offer camel markets, where you can roam between rows of rope-bridled camels looking for a new home. Dare to take one for a spin?

- **SIZE:** 63,170 sq mi (163,610 sq km)
- **POPULATION:** 11,135,000
- **CURRENCY:** Tunisian dinar
- **CAPITAL:** Tunis
- **LANGUAGE:** Arabic

Libya
AFRICA

* Brome grass, canary grass, bluegrass, and rye grass grow on Libya's coastal plains
* Tripoli's museum of history has an exhibit of former dictator Colonel Gaddafi's cars

Once a poor land of Berber nomads who roamed the Sahara desert, I struck it rich when gas companies drilled down to my oily depths in 1959. But in recent years, civil war has reduced my oil industry to a dribble.

In the days before Christianity, I was split in two: eastern Cyrenaica, colonized by the Phoenicians, and western Tripolitania, the province of the Greeks. Both regions became outposts of the Roman Empire; my Roman ruins in Leptis Magna feature ancient archways topped with huge heads of the monster Medusa. In my northeastern village oasis, Ghadames, age-old homes have been modeled from mud, lime, and palm tree trunks. Like honeycombed caves, they give protection from the brutal desert sun. The Ubari sand sea is a vast area of sculpted dunes with 20 palm-fringed, salty micro lakes; 200,000 years ago, the area was one enormous lake. At Al-Harüj al-Aswad at my center, remnants of ancient lava streams form a vast black, basalt plateau that rises 2600 feet (800 m) out of the sand.

SIZE: 679,362 sq mi (1,759,540 sq km)

POPULATION: 6,542,000

CURRENCY: Libyan dinar

CAPITAL: Tripoli

LANGUAGE: Arabic

95

Egypt

AFRICA

- ✳ The tomb of the young pharaoh Tutankhamen lay undiscovered for more than 3000 years
- ✳ The hunting dog of the pharaohs is related to today's Ibizan Hound dog breed

- ○ **SIZE:** 386,662 sq mi (1,001,450 sq km)
- ◉ **POPULATION:** 94,667,000
- ○ **CURRENCY:** Egyptian pound
- ◉ **CAPITAL:** Cairo
- ○ **LANGUAGE:** Arabic

Can I just say? I'm more than my ancient past! I'm like a rock star forced to replay the old hits. Spin the Sphinx again, baby! Man, play those Pyramids one more time.

I'm high tech, alright? I connected the Mediterranean and Red Seas by building the Suez Canal (in 1869) *and* I harnessed the Nile River by building the Aswan High Dam (opened 1970). To build the dam, which provides a renewable source of energy for electricity, my guys had to dig out 57 million cubic yards (44 million m³) of rubble and earth. They also had to dismantle my colossal Abu Simbel temple complex, rock by rock, to rebuild it on higher ground. Oh, and the practice of irrigation started on my land, when ancient Egyptians (yes, OK, those guys again) sowed seeds in muddy land left by the annual flooding of the Nile River.

Mauritania

AFRICA

Almost entirely desert, I'm the ancient route for trans-Saharan camel caravans, packing sacks of gold and dates to trade in my coastal capital. On the way, they'd have passed an oasis or two and the Guelb er Richat—a curious rock structure that looks like a bullseye from outer space. My old Islamic pilgrimage city, Chinguetti, is the site of the 13th-century Friday Mosque, with its simple, square stone minaret and treasure of medieval Islamic manuscripts.

○ **SIZE:** 397,955 sq mi (1,030,700 sq km)

◑ **POPULATION:** 3,677,000

○ **CURRENCY:** Mauritanian ouguiya

● **CAPITAL:** Nouakchott

○ **LANGUAGE:** Arabic

Senegal

AFRICA

I'm a country of rolling, sandy plains whose capital serves three key shipping lanes. The heron-friendly Senegal River forms a natural border to my north, and forest and mangrove swamps fringe my southern edge. Although my people are 90 percent Muslim, the influences of former French colonizers and Arabic North Africa have infused their culture. You'll see printed cotton fabrics styled into classic head wraps and flowing caftan-like robes.

○ **SIZE:** 75,955 sq mi (196,722 sq km)

◑ **POPULATION:** 14,320,000

○ **CURRENCY:** CFA franc

● **CAPITAL:** Dakar

○ **LANGUAGES:** French, Wolof

The Gambia

AFRICA

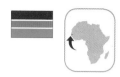

- ✻ Arab traders brought Islam to this country; today's population is 90 percent Muslim
- ✻ Apart from its short coastline, The Gambia is entirely surrounded by Senegal

- ○ **SIZE:** 4363 sq mi (11,300 sq km)
- ◉ **POPULATION:** 2,010,000
- ○ **CURRENCY:** Gambian dalasi
- ● **CAPITAL:** Banjul
- ○ **LANGUAGES:** English, Mandinka

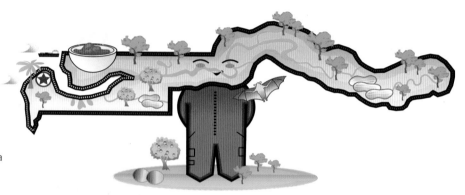

I resemble a wiggly finger rudely tickling Senegal's tummy. My territory borders both sides of the Gambia River as it meanders toward the Atlantic.

My poor soil quality means that most farming on my land is subsistence-level—people grow just enough food to eat. Peanuts are a major crop and feature in *domoda*, a stew made with peanut butter, tomato, chili pepper, pumpkin, and lemon. My namesake river is both a blessing and a curse. Navigable along its length, the river ends at Banjul, a bustling port on the Atlantic coast. In the 1700s, thousands of Africans were transported to the Americas from here, to work as slaves. If you take a twilight stroll along the river, look for Gambian epauletted fruit bats heading out to hang in the nearest mango grove. Their "epaulettes" are little tufts of hair on their shoulders.

Guinea-Bissau

AFRICA

A mostly low-lying, tropical, swamplike place, my land rises to grassland and forest in the east. To the west, my Bijagós archipelago features 88 offshore tropical islands—home to dolphins and manatees. I also attract 96 species of migratory birds. Big fishing fleets are scared off by the sand bars between my islands, so the solitary angler rules here. Cashew! No, I didn't sneeze, I'm just bragging about my major nutty export.

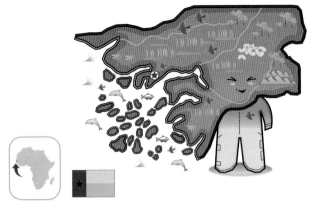

- ○ **SIZE:** 13,948 sq mi (36,125 sq km)
- ○ **POPULATION:** 1,760,000
- ○ **CURRENCY:** CFA franc
- ● **CAPITAL:** Bissau
- ○ **LANGUAGES:** Portuguese, Guineau-Bissau Creole

Guinea

AFRICA

A republic on the western coast of Africa, I have a patchwork terrain of coastal mangrove swamps yielding to flat grassy plains and both lowland and mountain forests alternating with savanna. My capital, on Tombo island, is linked to the Kaloum peninsula mainland by a causeway. Not only am I mineral rich, being chock-full of bauxite, but I'm one of Africa's wettest countries; my Mount Nimba nature reserve has 50 springs.

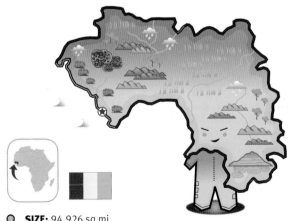

- ○ **SIZE:** 94,926 sq mi (245,857 sq km)
- ○ **POPULATION:** 12,093,000
- ○ **CURRENCY:** Guinean franc
- ● **CAPITAL:** Conakry
- ○ **LANGUAGE:** French

Sierra Leone

AFRICA

My long Atlantic coastline is backed by green hills lush with coconut and banana trees. In recent years, an outbreak of the deadly Ebola virus had devastating effects, but I am getting back on track. And I have much to be proud of: My capital, Freetown, was founded by freed slaves; in 2017, the generosity of my people was shown when a part-time diamond miner found a 706-carat diamond—and donated it to my treasury.

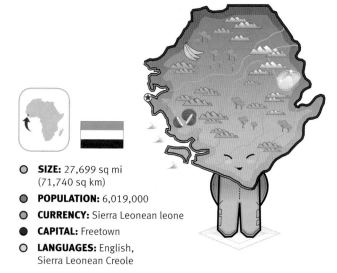

- ○ **SIZE:** 27,699 sq mi (71,740 sq km)
- ◍ **POPULATION:** 6,019,000
- ○ **CURRENCY:** Sierra Leonean leone
- ● **CAPITAL:** Freetown
- ○ **LANGUAGES:** English, Sierra Leonean Creole

Liberia

AFRICA

Founded in the early 19th century by freed slaves sent back from America, my name is a play on the word "liberty." From rolling plains along my coast, I'm a hilly place once you get inland, and I have a cluster of low mountains in my northeast. I'm rich in diamonds, iron ore, and timber. Europeans used to call me the Pepper Coast for my spicy malagueta pepper, once my main export.

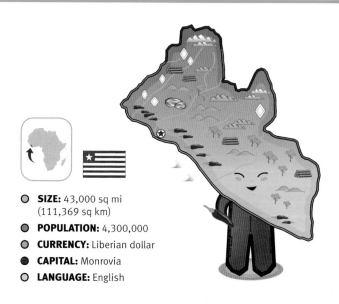

- ○ **SIZE:** 43,000 sq mi (111,369 sq km)
- ◍ **POPULATION:** 4,300,000
- ○ **CURRENCY:** Liberian dollar
- ● **CAPITAL:** Monrovia
- ○ **LANGUAGE:** English

Ivory Coast

AFRICA

※ French is the official language here, but over 70 indigenous languages are spoken

※ The Basilica of Our Lady of Peace in Yamoussoukro is the largest church in the world

Prince of pods—the world's premier producer of cocoa—I am a chocolate-maker's dream. I owe my status as West Africa's most profitable economy to cocoa beans, although I also produce coffee, rubber, sustainable palm oil, mahogany—and in the past, ivory from elephant tusks. I was once known as the Côte des Dents—"Coast of Teeth"—for my ivory chops!

Growing crops for export encourages deforestation—chopping down forests to make room for mono-cropping. It is a profitable business, so squatters steal and destroy my forest to grow cocoa illegally. And when forests disappear, so do my pygmy hippos, elephants, and pangolins, as well as colobus monkeys and many other primates. My people are creative, though. Korhogo cloth, made by the Senufo tribe, is handmade cotton painted with traditional symbols using fermented mud paint. And the beautiful wooden sculptures and masks of the Baule artisans influenced modern European artists such as Picasso and Modigliani.

- **SIZE:** 124,504 sq mi (322,463 sq km)
- **POPULATION:** 23,740,000
- **CURRENCY:** CFA franc
- **CAPITAL:** Yamoussoukro
- **LANGUAGE:** French

Ghana

AFRICA

☀ Lake Volta, the world's largest artificial lake, provides hydroelectric power

☀ The poisonous cobra and puff adder snakes are native to Ghana

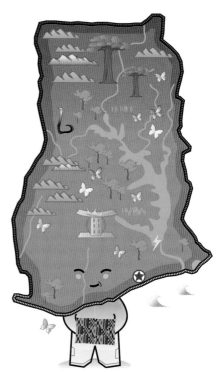

You could say I had the golden touch—my land was once the center of the famous Ashanti Empire, a West African tribal power at its height from the 17th to 19th centuries. Founder King Osei Tutu conquered other tribes and produced the Golden Stool, a kind of throne that he claimed had floated out of the sky and landed in his lap—a sign that he was the divinely anointed ruler! I was once known as the Gold Coast, and the Ashantis prospered by trading in gold and selling slaves. Their descendants are still my largest tribe.

Butterflies. More than 650 species of the winged beauties flutter over my land—twice the number found in Europe. Baobabs. My people love those trees of mine, eating their gourd-like fruit and making barrels from their trunks. They even fashion clothing from the bark. And baskets. Kente cloth is a traditional textile art of my Ashanti and Ewe tribes. The name Kente means "basket," referring to the interweaving of vibrantly colored, geometric-patterned strips.

○ **SIZE:** 92,098 sq mi (239,000 sq km)

◐ **POPULATION:** 26,908,262

◑ **CURRENCY:** Ghanaian cedi

● **CAPITAL:** Accra

○ **LANGUAGE:** English

Togo

AFRICA

A thin slip of a country, I'm mostly marshy mangroves to my south and tropical savanna to my north—expect to see an elephant or a leopard. My Mono River runs down at least two-thirds of my length. I'm a bit murky (in Ewe language, my name means "land where lagoons lie"), but primitive? Hardly. Sophisticated scholars of earth-friendly architecture scurry here to study my *takienta*, the mud tower houses of my Batammariba people.

- **SIZE:** 21,925 sq mi (56,785 sq km)
- **POPULATION:** 7,757,000
- **CURRENCY:** CFA franc
- **CAPITAL:** Lomé
- **LANGUAGE:** French

Benin

AFRICA

L ike Togo, I'm narrow with a short, mangrove coastline. The Mono River acts as a boundary between us to the south and we share the Atakora mountain range to my northeast. In my city of Ouidah, my Temple of the Sacred Python—full of free-wriggling reptiles—commemorates a legend that describes forest pythons protecting my ancient King Kpassé during a war. French cabaret meets Congolese rumba in the folk music of my people.

- **SIZE:** 43,484 sq mi (112,622 sq km)
- **POPULATION:** 10,741,000
- **CURRENCY:** CFA franc
- **CAPITAL:** Porto-Novo
- **LANGUAGE:** French

Burkina Faso

AFRICA

* Burkina Faso's Nazinga Reserve has the largest elephant population in West Africa
* Bwa masqueraders in black-and-white masks dance at harvest and funeral ceremonies

- **SIZE:** 105,869 sq mi (274,200 sq km)
- **POPULATION:** 19,513,000
- **CURRENCY:** CFA franc
- **CAPITAL:** Ouagadougou
- **LANGUAGE:** French

A landlocked former French colony, my climate is arid and hot, my soil is poor, and I'm subject to that most ancient of plagues: the desert locust. Still, I usually take the annual prize as Africa's most productive producer of cotton!

My village of Tiébélé, home to the royal court of the Kassena ethnic group since the 15th century, is famed for its earthen homes built from a mush of mud, straw, cow dung, and chalk. Strengthened with a "secret-sauce" varnish made from locust beans, the structures are elaborately painted with vibrant symbolic designs. The villagescape includes mausoleums, as the dead are laid to rest inside the village walls. Elsewhere, my people work to the bouncing beat of *balafons*, or get down to *djembes*—just a few of my traditionally crafted drums.

Mali

AFRICA

* To the north of Mali lies the Sahara desert; to the south is tropical savanna
* A large sandstone mound, La Main de Fatima, resembles an upraised hand

My story majors on sun, sand, and salt. In the old days of the Mali Empire (13th–16th centuries), nomadic Tuareg traders in salt, gold, silk, and slaves clambered onto camels to travel in caravans between my fabled trading post Timbuktu, on the Niger River, and Mediterranean ports. The Tuaregs were known as the "blue people" because they used my native *Indigofera* plant to dye their robes and turbans. (It also dyed their skin blue!)

My Dogon people have inhabited the Bandiagara escarpment since Paleolithic times. Set into the rocks, their cavelike dwellings have neither electricity nor plumbing! These spiritual people are known for their incredible rock art and for a ritualistic funeral dance that features masks towering 2 feet (60 cm) high. Interaction with people from the Middle East brought the Islamic faith. Today, Djenné, an ancient center of Islamic learning, is home to the Great Mosque, the world's largest mud-brick building.

○ **SIZE:** 478,841 sq mi (1,240,192 sq km)

◑ **POPULATION:** 17,467,000

○ **CURRENCY:** CFA franc

● **CAPITAL:** Bamako

○ **LANGUAGES:** French, Bambara

Niger

AFRICA

- Remains of a 110-million-year-old "Super Croc" fossil were found in the Ténéré desert
- Roasted locusts and camel milk yogurt feature in Niger's desert cuisine

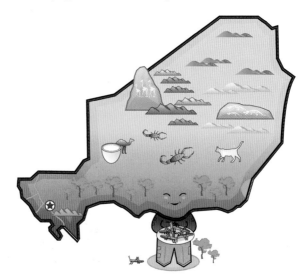

SIZE: 489,191 sq mi
(1,267,000 sq km)

POPULATION:
18,639,000

CURRENCY:
CFA franc

CAPITAL:
Niamey

LANGUAGE:
French

Known for desert, drought, and deadly wildlife, I'm home to the deathstalker scorpion and the horned sand viper—both venomous. But did you know I also have my very own sand cat? It's an adorable domestic-looking kitty, with thick hair covering its footpads to protect them from the hot sand.

My Air and Ténéré Reserves, two linked desert regions, offer extraordinary evidence of a greener prehistoric past. In the Air Mountains, highly detailed, 18-foot- (5.5-m-) tall petroglyphs of giraffes suggest that, 6000 years ago, enough foliage grew here for these herbivores to prosper. In my Ténéré desert, today a stark land of sand, numerous human skeletons have been found in an ancient burial ground. Pollen evidence suggests that some of the bodies were laid to rest on beds of flowers.

Nigeria
AFRICA

✳ Nigeria is known for the "afrobeat" music of Fela Kuti, a songwriter and political activist
✳ Native Cross River gorillas and Nigeria–Cameroon chimpanzees are endangered species

L ights, camera, action! I'm made for the spotlights—life in the slow lane is not my style. I'm Africa's most populous country—Lagos, my largest city, is home to 21 million people. They all need to be kept amused, and I deliver: Nollywood, my film industry, makes more films per year than Hollywood.

My people have stratospheric style—you only need to look at the gravity-defying head wraps (*geles*) beloved of Nigerian women to see that. Even my oil—I'm the world's sixth-largest producer of petroleum—is a star: Known as "light sweet crude," it needs very little refining. America is one of my biggest customers: I'm running your wheels and warming your butts, guys!

My Niger River—Africa's third longest—forms a web of tributaries known as the Niger Delta before it flows into the Gulf of Guinea. The delta's mangrove swamps and rain forests are where my wildlife hang out—monkeys, crocodiles, snakes, turtles, and fish.

○ **SIZE:** 356,669 sq mi (923,768 sq km)
○ **POPULATION:** 186,053,000
○ **CURRENCY:** Nigerian naira
● **CAPITAL:** Abuja
○ **LANGUAGE:** English

107

Chad

AFRICA

* Elaborately engraved calabashes (gourds) are a traditional Chadian art
* Chad has more than 200 ethnic groups speaking over 100 languages

Landlocked, I have a northern Sahara desert region and a central belt of Sahel savanna that depend on a rainy season that is a lot less reliable than it used to be!

My Sahara desert is home to the Ounianga Lakes and the Ennedi Massif, two landscapes of startling beauty. The Ennedi's eroded sandstone rock formations look like they were imported from the planet Mars. Then there are the freshwater lakes—18 lake oases in the middle of the Sahara, fed by underground springs. If only my Lake Chad were so lucky. Once the world's sixth-largest lake, poor Lake Chad has shrunk by over 90 percent from its 1963 level. I blame climate change and the demands of my growing population for water to irrigate crops. Elsewhere, I have valuable resources—oil and, in my northern Tibesti mountains (extinct volcanoes, the highest elevations in the Sahara), geothermal springs, minerals, and metals such as uranium, tungsten, and natron (the salt that the ancient Egyptians used to dry mummies).

- **SIZE:** 495,755 sq mi (1,284,000 sq km)
- **POPULATION:** 11,852,000
- **CURRENCY:** CFA franc
- **CAPITAL:** N'Djamena
- **LANGUAGES:** Arabic, French

Cameroon
AFRICA

Coast, savanna, desert, rain forest, mountains—it's all here, plus at least 250 ethnic tribes who speak over 270 languages. My traditional homes include cooling Musgum mud huts inscribed with beautifully detailed patterns and, in the rain forest, bark huts with conical thatched roofs. My drill monkeys—so shy—are hard to miss as they flee deep into the rain forest, their retreating backsides flashing mauve, pink, and blue.

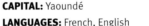

- **SIZE:** 183,568 sq mi (475,440 sq km)
- **POPULATION:** 24,361,000
- **CURRENCY:** CFA franc
- **CAPITAL:** Yaoundé
- **LANGUAGES:** French, English

Equatorial Guinea
AFRICA

My landscape features coastal volcanic islands and the Rio Muni rain forest. My most populous ethnic group is the Bantu-speaking Fang; fierce jungle fighters, famed for a call-and-response-style music played on the *tam tam*, an animal-skin drum, and the *mvet*, a bamboo harp. The black volcanic sand of my Ureca beaches attracts sea turtles, come egg-laying time. Even in my capital nature rules: check out the 230-foot- (70-m-) high silk cotton trees.

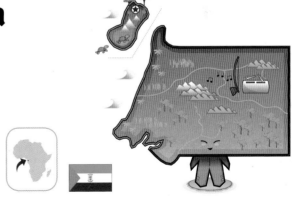

- **SIZE:** 10,831 sq mi (28,051 sq km)
- **POPULATION:** 759,000
- **CURRENCY:** CFA franc
- **CAPITAL:** Malabo
- **LANGUAGES:** Spanish, French

Central African Republic

AFRICA

Landlocked, I lie at Africa's geographic center. Well-watered by the Ubangi and Sangha rivers, my northern savanna gives way to dense tropical rain forest in the south. My hunter-gatherer people, the BaAka, retain the impressive survival talents of early humans, skilled at hunting with nets, poison-tipped arrows, and crossbows. And they have a rich variety of wildlife to stalk: monkeys, antelopes, and crocodiles for starters.

- **SIZE:** 240,353 sq mi (622,984 sq km)
- **POPULATION:** 5,507,000
- **CURRENCY:** CFA franc
- **CAPITAL:** Bangui
- **LANGUAGES:** French, Sango

Congo

AFRICA

Slashed in two by the Equator and bordered by the Congo River, mine is a sparsely populated land with a short coastline to the southwest. Clever chimps in my Goualougo Triangle rain forest show that they are masters at using tools, such as slender, sharp sticks to penetrate termite nests. According to legend, the Mokele-Mbembe—a giant reptile—lurks in my fearsome Likouala Swamp, an area of 54,000 square miles (140,000 sq km).

- **SIZE:** 132,047 sq mi (342,000 sq km)
- **POPULATION:** 4,852,000
- **CURRENCY:** CFA franc
- **CAPITAL:** Brazzaville
- **LANGUAGE:** French

Gabon

AFRICA

* Tribal leaders wear elaborate masks to perform traditional rituals and ceremonies
* Birdwatchers flock to Lake Oguemoué in the hope of spotting an African finfoot

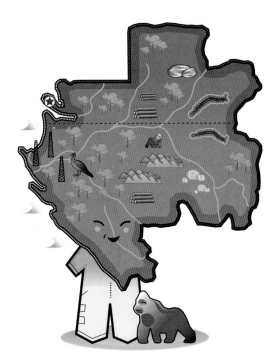

Neatly cut in half by the Equator, my terrain is a happy mash-up of coastal lagoons, mountain ranges, savanna, and lush rain forest. The Ogooué River cuts across my middle, spreading tentacles of tributaries through my interior reaches. My capital city, Libreville (Freetown), was founded by slaves liberated by the French Navy from a Brazilian slave ship. Africa's least densely populated country, I'm richly resourced—I've got a long Atlantic coastline with white sand beaches, oil, timber, manganese, gold, and iron.

The first European sighting of a gorilla (in 1856, by the French zoologist Paul Du Chaillu) was made on my land; hardly surprising given my possession of Earth's second-largest jungle zone. And my bugs are ablaze! Well, not exactly, but they do glow in the dark. My fire centipedes are bioluminescent—they light up when you touch them . . . but watch out, these critters' bites are full of venom!

SIZE: 103,347 sq mi (267,667 sq km)

POPULATION: 1,739,000

CURRENCY: CFA franc

CAPITAL: Libreville

LANGUAGE: French

Democratic Republic of the Congo

AFRICA

* Kinshasa and Congo's capital Brazzaville sit opposite each other on the Congo River
* Natural resources include diamonds, cobalt, copper, and petroleum

Wow! Where to start? Everywhere you look, you'll find some kind of natural marvel. Take the mighty Congo River—Africa's second largest—which winds its way across the continent, its amazing journey ending at my Matadi port. Or maybe I can tempt you to visit one of my nine enormous nature reserves to see giraffes, okapis, hippos, rhinos, and forest elephants roaming wild. Up high, you'll see the peak of my glowing stratovolcano, Mount Nyiragongo, a steaming lava lake filling its center. Down below, you'll find mines dug for cobalt minerals—your i-Phone won't charge without them. Rumor has it my streams are laced with diamonds; for sure, mountain gorillas inhabit my lush rain forests.

Sounds idyllic, I know, but life here is hard. Only nine percent of my 65 million people have electricity at home. The animals in my nature reserves are in danger from poachers. And sometimes children get sent to work in the cobalt mines instead of going to school.

○ **SIZE:** 905,358 sq mi (2,344,858 sq km)

○ **POPULATION:** 81,331,000

○ **CURRENCY:** Congolese franc

● **CAPITAL:** Kinshasa

○ **LANGUAGE:** French

Sudan

AFRICA

Before 2011 and my break with South Sudan, I was Africa's largest country, an ancient Nubian civilization known as Kush, lying where the Blue and White Nile rivers meet. I boast more pyramids than Egypt in my Meroe and Nuri deserts! In Karima, my tabletop mountain, Jebel Barkal, is the legendary home of the ancient Egyptian god Amun. But don't get caught up in my desert sandstorm *haboob*, a blinding cloud of swirling dust.

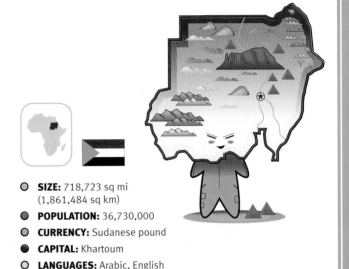

- **SIZE:** 718,723 sq mi (1,861,484 sq km)
- **POPULATION:** 36,730,000
- **CURRENCY:** Sudanese pound
- **CAPITAL:** Khartoum
- **LANGUAGES:** Arabic, English

South Sudan

AFRICA

Rich with oil, I'm still underdeveloped, thanks to decades of civil war. My vast Sudd Swamp, where the White Nile spills over into my wide basin grasslands, offers a refuge for crocodiles lurking in papyrus marshes and migrating elephant herds. The Imatong Mountains on my Ugandan border serve as a water reserve for my capital. In my Boma region live the Suri people, pastoral cow herders known for their ritual *donga* (stick fights).

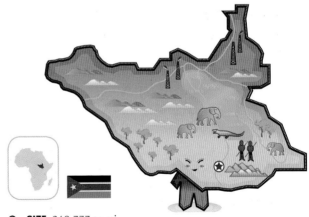

- **SIZE:** 248,777 sq mi (644,329 sq km)
- **POPULATION:** 12,531,000
- **CURRENCY:** South Sudanese pound
- **CAPITAL:** Juba
- **LANGUAGE:** English

Eritrea

AFRICA

My capital, Asmara, showcases 1930s-era Art Deco architecture, a legacy from my time as an Italian colony. I sit on the Afar Triangle, where three of Earth's tectonic plates meet up to rumble: Active underground volcanoes spew magma that rises through my crust, hardens, and sinks, lowering my land. *Teff* anyone? This staple food is one of several crops grown here; agriculture employs 80 percent of my population.

- **SIZE:** 45,406 sq. mi. (117,600 sq km)
- **POPULATION:** 5,870,000
- **CURRENCY:** Eritrean nakfa
- **CAPITAL:** Asmara
- **LANGUAGES:** Tigrinya, Arabic, English

Djibouti

AFRICA

Craving a salty snack? Try an Afar salt pearl—spheres of salt dug from my Lac Assal, the continent's lowest elevation. My Afar people, known for their butter-sculpted dreadlocks, have for centuries led camel caravans across the lake to collect salt to trade. Ancient forests in my north give way to desert plains, while Lake Abbe, on my western border, fronts a landscape of tall limestone smokestacks belching sulfurous steam jets.

- **SIZE:** 8958 sq mi (23,200 sq km)
- **POPULATION:** 847,000
- **CURRENCY:** Djiboutian franc
- **CAPITAL:** Djibouti City
- **LANGUAGES:** French, Arabic

Somalia

AFRICA

* Livestock counts toward Somalia's main exports: cattle, sheep, goats, and camels
* Cows with large horns feature in ancient cave paintings at Laas Gaal (9000 B.C.E.)

Someday, I'm going to be a superstar. With my palm-tree-lined coastline—Africa's longest—it should be a cinch!

You won't get farther east than me on this continent; a peninsula on the eastern "horn" of Africa, I jut into the Indian Ocean. Apart from the Cal Madow mountain range in my northeast, my landscape remains remarkably flat and desertlike. This, combined with an extremely arid climate, makes it hard to grow food and harsh famines are not uncommon.

My people are known for their elegant features, their rich story-telling tradition, their exotic trades, and a cuisine that betrays Southeast Asian influences. They climb rocky cliffs to search for wild frankincense trees so they can scrape out the precious, fragrant resin. My Islamic heritage is ancient: The Fakhr-al-Din Mosque (1269) in my capital Mogadishu is built of coral blocks and features two blue minarets, side by side, one dome-shaped and one cone-shaped.

- **SIZE:** 246,201 sq mi (637,657 sq km)
- **POPULATION:** 10,817,000
- **CURRENCY:** Somali shilling
- **CAPITAL:** Mogadishu
- **LANGUAGES:** Somali, Arabic

Ethiopia

AFRICA

* In 1972, a 3.2-million-year-old hominid skeleton, "Lucy," was unearthed in the Rift Valley
* The Ethiopian wolf is the world's most endangered member of the dog family

- **SIZE:** 426,373 sq mi
  (1,104,300 sq km)
- **POPULATION:**
  102,374,000
- **CURRENCY:**
  Ethiopian birr
- **CAPITAL:**
  Addis Ababa
- **LANGUAGES:** Oromo,
  Amharic

The earliest known fossils of *Homo sapiens* were found right here—that fills me with pride. The Rift Valley slices through my highly elevated central plateau, sometimes called the roof of Africa; seven alkaline lakes pool within the canyon formed by the rift. My Danakil Depression, the lowest, hottest place in Africa, is formed by two separating tectonic plates. It'll cool off someday when the split gets so wide that the Red Sea spills in!

My famous eleven Lalibela churches were cut (in the 12th century) out of volcanic rock. Visit the church at Aksum, the ruins of an ancient trading city on my northern border. According to legend, the church harbors the ark of the covenant—a chest that holds the original stone tablet with the ten commandments of the Jewish, Islamic, and Christian faiths: monks guard the ark and are said not to leave their post until their death.

* Among Kenya's biggest exports are tea, flowers, and coffee
* Kenya is well known for its middle- and long-distance runners

SIZE: 224,081 sq mi
(580,367 sq km)

POPULATION:
46,790,000

CURRENCY:
Kenyan shilling

CAPITAL:
Nairobi

LANGUAGES:
English, Kiswahili

What did I do to deserve me? When it comes to standout features, I rule! Ports? My port city Mombasa, basking on a coral island in the Indian Ocean, is so desirable that in Kiswahili it was known as "Island of War." The Portuguese, Arabs, Omanis, and Zimba tribe have all battled for it. Mountains? Mount Kenya—an extinct volcano—splattered with remnant glaciers is the legendary throne of Ngai, high god of my Kikuyu tribe. And I guarantee my Rift Valley, formed around 20 million years ago, offers an otherworldly landscape visible from the International Space Station!

My Maasai Mara is stuffed with prey: zebras, impalas, and gazillions of gazelles—heaven for prowling big cat predators. Nairobi, my very 21st-century capital city (otherwise known as the Silicon Savanna), is big on cellphone technology, which is great for nomads. And just south of Nairobi, I'm developing Konza Tech City, soon to be my national high-tech hub.

Uganda

AFRICA

* Lake Victoria is the world's second-largest freshwater lake
* Black-and-white colobus monkeys inhabit Entebbe's botanical gardens

I'm for the birds—they keep my spirits aloft. And with my stable, warm, wet equatorial climate and lush forests, birds just love me. I'm home to over 1000 avian species, including the great blue turaco (a dude sporting a serious midnight-blue flattop) and my national bird: the East African crowned crane, whose courtship dance moves feature fancy feats of flapping, twirling, and foot stomping. My Bwindi Impenetrable Forest is home to 160 species of vine-hung trees and half the world's mountain gorilla population.

I have more lakes than any other African country. They include Lake Victoria, which I share with Tanzania and Kenya. To the west, along my Congo River border, lower slopes of my misty, snow-capped Rwenzori Mountains are cushioned by moorland and festooned with ferns, lichens, and giant lobelia flowers. In my southwestern foothills, seminomadic cattle herders treasure their native Ankole cattle—an ancient breed whose curved horns can measure 8 feet (2.4 m) from tip to tip.

- **SIZE:** 93,065 sq mi (241,038 sq km)
- **POPULATION:** 38,319,000
- **CURRENCY:** Ugandan shilling
- **CAPITAL:** Kampala
- **LANGUAGE:** English

Rwanda

AFRICA

Allow me to introduce myself as one of Africa's most pleasant and prosperous countries—a land of green hills, mountains, forests, and savannas— plus a place in which plastic bags are banned! Everything grows well here: tea, coffee, sweet potatoes, bananas, and cassava. Among my residents are primates—silverback gorillas, golden monkeys—and you'll find human primates, too: the Tutsi, Hutu, and Twa peoples.

- ○ **SIZE:** 10,169 sq mi (26,338 sq km)
- ◓ **POPULATION:** 12,988,000
- ○ **CURRENCY:** Rwandan franc
- ● **CAPITAL:** Kigali
- ○ **LANGUAGES:** Kinyarwanda, French, English

Burundi

AFRICA

So I'm small, but I also have one jaw-dropping claim to fame: The great Nile River starts here. Yep, in a little hidden spring on my Mount Kikizi. Impressed? You will be when you see my gorgeous triple-cascade Kagera Falls. And don't miss out on my mystical drumming tradition! My Royal Drummers perform at royal funerals and feasts. Their drums are stored like precious jewels in sanctuaries located in sacred groves.

- ○ **SIZE:** 10,745 sq mi (27,830 sq km)
- ◓ **POPULATION:** 11,099,000
- ○ **CURRENCY:** Burundian franc
- ● **CAPITAL:** Bujumbura
- ○ **LANGUAGES:** Kirundi, French, English

Tanzania

AFRICA

※ Tanzania's Serengeti National Park is home to huge herds of gazelles and zebras

※ A Maasai tribesman discovered blue tanzanite in Mount Kilimanjaro's foothills

Two countries merged to form me in 1964, leaving me the legacy of their names, Tanganyika and Zanzibar. Exotic names rule: Dar es Salaam, my Indian Ocean port city, means "abode of peace" in Arabic.

Around three million years ago, one of my volcanoes collapsed inward to form my Ngorongoro Crater, a region now home to Africa's densest concentration of "big five" game: lion, leopard, elephant, Cape buffalo, and rhino. Just west of the collapsed crater in Laetoli, an 80-foot (23-m) trail of three-million-year-old ashy footprints helped archaeologists decide just when humans began to walk upright on two feet.

African violets and impatiens, two of the world's most common house and yard plants, are native to my shady, humid Usambara Mountains. Mount Kilimanjaro, the world's highest free-standing mountain, is really a million-year-old heap of hardened volcanic ash, lava, pumice, and tephra (rock fragments).

- **SIZE:** 365,755 sq mi (947,300 sq km)
- **POPULATION:** 52,483,000
- **CURRENCY:** Tanzanian shilling
- **CAPITAL:** Dodoma
- **LANGUAGES:** English, Swahili

Malawi
AFRICA

I'm known as the "warm heart of Africa" and for the sunrises and sunsets reflected over my deep Lake Malawi. It also goes by the name, Calendar Lake, because it's *365* miles (587 km) long, *52* miles (84 km) wide, and fed by *12* rivers. Its waters teem with a kaleidoscopic collection of neon-colored cichlids (fish). Time for tea? While the rest of Africa is hooked on coffee plantations, I prefer tea: I was the first African country to grow it commercially.

- **SIZE:** 45,747 sq mi (118,484 sq km)
- **POPULATION:** 18,570,000
- **CURRENCY:** Malawian kwacha
- **CAPITAL:** Lilongwe
- **LANGUAGE:** English, Chichewa

Angola
AFRICA

I have oil and diamonds to boost my economy and a topography that varies wildly from flat coastal plain to steeply rising tablelands and cliffs. My interior is dominated by a high-elevation plateau. Even daredevil drivers quake at the thought of my Serra Da Leba Pass road, a series of 12 serpentine swerves with no guard rails! My national bird, the red-crested turaco, provides a splash of color, with its green feathers, blue tail, and bright-red crest.

- **SIZE:** 481,354 sq mi (1,246,700 sq km)
- **POPULATION:** 20,172,000
- **CURRENCY:** Angolan kwanza
- **CAPITAL:** Luanda
- **LANGUAGE:** Portuguese

Mozambique

AFRICA

- Maputo's colonial buildings include a mint-green rail station with a wrought-iron dome
- The Zambezi River, with its Cahora Bassa dam, provides irrigation for tea and sugar crops

Tourists, come spread your beach towels on my white sands! My civil war ended in 1992 and my Portuguese colonizers finally moved on. So now I am cultivating a beachy paradise vibe. Coral reefs and island archipelagos fringe my tropical, 1550-mile (2500-km) coastline. In the Mozambique Channel off my coast, you can surf, snorkel, sail (*dhows*, slim-hulled Arab boats, are traditional), or reel in marlin, kingfish, and sailfish.

My terrain consists mostly of flat coastal plains—easy on the flip-flops—that is, until you penetrate my interior. The 16,200-square-mile (42,000-sq-km) Lake Niassa reserve on my north central border is part of the East African plateau. It features miombo (a type of tree) woodland and wetlands. Lethal black mamba snakes lurk in the rocky, eroded hillocks that rise abruptly from the plain, while lions, leopards, elephants, wildebeests, and zebras roam the forests. A large population of African wild dogs keeps poachers at bay.

- **SIZE:** 308,642 sq mi (799,380 sq km)
- **POPULATION:** 25,930,000
- **CURRENCY:** Mozambique metical
- **CAPITAL:** Maputo
- **LANGUAGE:** Portuguese

Namibia

AFRICA

* The San speak a click language that uses clicking sounds for about five consonants
* Namibia's diamond mines supply almost 30 percent of the world diamonds

Awesome? I think I am. The word means imposing, stirring, stunning, and all of these apply to my Namib and Kalahari desert landscapes, and to the hunter-gatherer culture of my San people.

I'm a land of deserts. In my coastal Namib desert (the world's oldest), the Sossusvlei sand dunes (the world's tallest) constantly change shape due to winds. Iron oxide in the sand makes them red. It's a foggy place: The Atlantic's Benguela current interacts with the ocean to send mist inland. Everything living in my severe scapes adapts for water scarcity: The bandit-masked, spear-horned oryx (a type of antelope) sucks water from succulent desert plants. The *Welwitschia mirabilis* plant grows only two long strappy leaves aboveground, but a very long, deep tap root. In the inland Kalahari desert on my Botswanan border stands the quiver tree, a species of aloe. It is so-named because my hunter-gatherer San people hollow its branches to make quivers for their poison-tipped arrows.

○ **SIZE:** 318,261 sq mi (824,292 sq km)

○ **POPULATION:** 2,436,000

○ **CURRENCY:** Namibian dollar

● **CAPITAL:** Windhoek

○ **LANGUAGE:** English

Zambia

AFRICA

※ Giant termite mounds of rich red soil pepper Zambia's plateau areas

※ The small, native Zambian barbet snaps its bill to make a loud clicking sound

A butterfly-shaped beauty at the heart of the continent, I take my name from the Zambezi River that crosses my southwest corner. Allow me to brag (eight million straw-colored fruit bats agree): My winey waterberries and sweet mangoes are fabulous. During their annual November migration, the bats feast in my Kasanka National Park. They form the largest gathering of fruit bats in the world, spreading the seeds of these rain-forest species in their purple poop.

That whooshing noise you hear is not beating batwings, but Victoria Falls. A spectacular waterfall known locally as "the smoke that thunders," it forms part of my border with Zimbabwe. Torrents of foamy H_2O hurtle some 355 feet (110 m) down into my Zambezi River gorge every second. During the dry season, the water diminishes just enough to allow risk-takers to bathe in Devil's Pool at the fall's edge—there's just a natural rock lip between the pool partygoers and the long drop.

○ **SIZE:** 290,587 sq mi (752,618 sq km)

◐ **POPULATION:** 15,511,000

○ **CURRENCY:** Zambian kwacha

● **CAPITAL:** Lusaka

○ **LANGUAGES:** English, Bembe

Zimbabwe

AFRICA

* Prehistoric paintings of elephants and giraffes grace cave walls in the Matobo Hills
* Tobacco and gold are among Zimbabwe's biggest exports

- **SIZE:** 150,872 sq mi (390,757 sq km)
- **POPULATION:** 14,547,000
- **CURRENCY:** US dollar
- **CAPITAL:** Harare
- **LANGUAGES:** Shona, Ndebele, English

My name translates as "big houses of stone," after the fortifications of what was once Great Zimbabwe—the center of my ancient Shona civilization. The walls of its 11th-century fortress were crowned with sculptures of my emblem, the bateleur eagle.

Once known as Southern Rhodesia, my journey out of the clutches of colonization has been hard fought, but like my capital, known for its vivid red flame trees and purple jacarandas, I still blossom with life and color. The grassy *vleis* and wetlands of my Mana Pools and Hwange reserves shelter healthy populations of nearly every type of African wildlife. My Matobo Hill country is known for its wind-smoothed rock formations. And lurking in the musically named Limpopo River on my South African border, cranky crocodiles bide their time, waiting for prey.

Botswana

AFRICA

* A 1109-carat diamond discovered in 2015 is called *Lesedi La Rona* ("our light")
* Botswana's national dish is *seswaa*, a stew of meat, maize meal, and greens

Rocks to riches! Diamonds are my business, and they've been good to me. Thanks to my responsible management of diamond profits, the percentage of my people in poverty has declined from 50 percent to 19 percent. Fills me with pride!

Meanwhile, back in my Okavango Delta, my people pole their *mokoro* canoes (hollowed from tree trunks) through the shallow waters and observe the wildlife scene. It's a cast of thousands: the striped, termite-eating aardwolves, hippos, lions, giraffes, meerkats, Cape buffalo, gnus, and cheetahs. My Chobe National Park is famed for its bird species including the malachite kingfisher, known for its incredible headfirst dives.

And diamonds aren't my only white mineral: My Makgadikgadi salt pan, an area the size of Switzerland, is known for its thousands of flamingos during flood season and for Chapman's baobab, a tree so large that explorers used it as a navigation beacon.

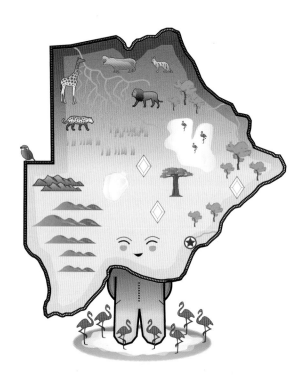

- **SIZE:** 224,607 sq mi (581,730 sq km)
- **POPULATION:** 2,209,000
- **CURRENCY:** Botswana pula
- **CAPITAL:** Gaborone
- **LANGUAGES:** English, Setswana

Lesotho

AFRICA

No, you are not in Switzerland, but in Lesotho—the roof of Africa. Mostly rugged Maloti Mountains, I'm known for my cool climate and Alpine fauna! Snow is common here. Due to my chill, my traditional clothing is cozy, patterned wool blanket wraps, and my huts are made of stone blocks instead of African clay or mud. Saving the best for last . . . I have my own pony, the fearless Basotho pony, named for one of my native tribes.

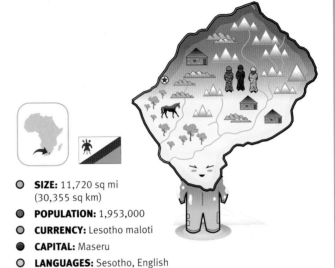

- **SIZE:** 11,720 sq mi (30,355 sq km)
- **POPULATION:** 1,953,000
- **CURRENCY:** Lesotho maloti
- **CAPITAL:** Maseru
- **LANGUAGES:** Sesotho, English

Swaziland

AFRICA

Made up of forest, savanna, and grassland, my territory is blessed with super-rich soil. No fewer than 2600 species of flowering plants and ferns grow here. Some, including *Kniphofia umbrina* (red-hot poker), are unique to my land. I'm big on ceremonies! For Incwala, a first-fruits celebration, men dress as warriors. Umhlanga is a reed dance—maidens dress in beaded skirts and ankle bracelets, gather reeds, and dance for my royalty.

- **SIZE:** 6704 sq mi (17,364 sq km)
- **POPULATION:** 1,451,000
- **CURRENCY:** Swaziland lilangeni
- **CAPITAL:** Mbabane
- **LANGUAGES:** English, siSwati

South Africa

AFRICA

- ✵ Flat-topped Table Mountain is one of Cape Town's most recognized landmarks
- ✵ The game animals—lion, elephant, rhino, Cape buffalo, leopard—feature on bank bills
- ✵ South Africa is the world's largest producer of gold

I get shivers when I think about it: My Cape Agulhas marks the southernmost point of this great African continent. The red-and-white lighthouse on my rocky headland looks out to the meeting of the Atlantic and Indian Oceans. Most of my land sits some 3300–6900 feet (1000–2100 m) up on a huge plateau, flanked to the east, south, and west by a series of mountain ranges collectively known as the Great Escarpment. That big hole? That's where you'll find Lesotho—totally surrounded.

My land benefits from the winds and currents of both the Atlantic (west) and Indian (east) oceans, resulting in biodiversity that is richer than the Amazon rain forest! Eighteen thousand plant species grow in my *fynbos* region—80 percent of them unique! My animals range from the geometric tortoise to the Cape sugar bird. Every May, millions of sardines migrate to my shores off KwaZulu-Natal, pursued hotly by hungry sharks, seals, dolphins, and humpback whales.

Besides my capital, Pretoria, important cities include coastal Cape Town (my parliament sits here) and Bloemfontein, home to my Supreme Court. I think of these cities as capitals, too. My financial center, Johannesburg, sprouted from a gold rush.

- ○ **SIZE:** 470,693 sq mi (1,219,090 sq km)
- ○ **POPULATION:** 54,301,000
- ○ **CURRENCY:** South African rand
- ● **CAPITAL:** Pretoria
- ○ **LANGUAGES:** IsiZulu, IsiXhosa, Afrikaans, English, Sepedi, Setswana, Sesotho, Xitsonga, siSwati, Tshivenda, isiNdebele

Apartheid ("Apartness")

Racial separation played a large role in South African politics during the 20th century, affecting all areas of society. It did not end until 1994, when the country elected its first black president, Nelson Mandela.

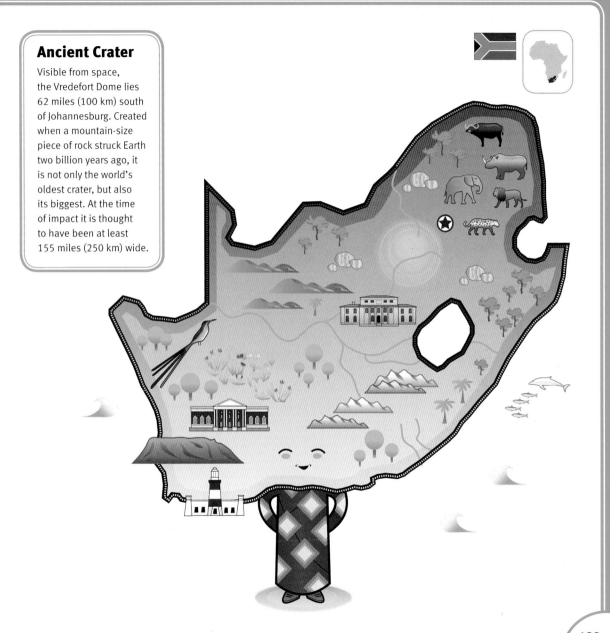

Ancient Crater

Visible from space, the Vredefort Dome lies 62 miles (100 km) south of Johannesburg. Created when a mountain-size piece of rock struck Earth two billion years ago, it is not only the world's oldest crater, but also its biggest. At the time of impact it is thought to have been at least 155 miles (250 km) wide.

Cape Verde

AFRICA

I'm an Atlantic archipelago of volcanic islands. Each one is different—from cinder heaps to lush banana and sugar-cane plantations. People even lived inside the crater of Pico, an active volcano, in huts made of volcanic rock. They grew wine in its fertile soil . . . until a 2014 eruption destroyed the village. I have a thriving dive scene: Once a port of call for shipping, now my 70 undersea shipwrecks create a murky maze for scuba divers.

- ○ **SIZE:** 1557 sq mi (4033 sq km)
- ◉ **POPULATION:** 553,000
- ○ **CURRENCY:** Cape Verdean escudo
- ● **CAPITAL:** Praia
- ○ **LANGUAGES:** Portuguese, Cape Verdean Creole

São Tomé & Príncipe

AFRICA

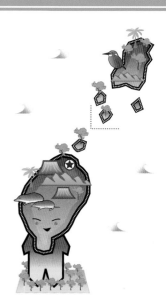

Two tiny volcanic islands off Africa's west coast, we claim rich volcanic soil, idyllic beaches, and good fishing among our riches, amid mountainous landscapes engulfed by rampant rain forest. Our indigenous creatures include the long-eared shrew and the malachite kingfisher. For dramatic flair you won't beat Auto de Floripes—a street-theater fest with great costumes and reenactments of medieval battles between Christians and Moors.

- ○ **SIZE:** 372 sq mi (964 sq km)
- ◉ **POPULATION:** 198,000
- ○ **CURRENCY:** STP dobra
- ● **CAPITAL:** São Tomé
- ○ **LANGUAGES:** Portuguese, Forro

Madagascar

AFRICA

* Rice, a major export, grows on terraces in the valleys of the central highlands
* The Rova, or King's Palace, stands on the capital's highest hill

Watch out! My tomato frog is so plump and red, you might accidentally put one on a pizza. Bad idea: They excrete a kind of glue. I'm a combined temperate and tropical Indian Ocean island, east of Mozambique. Around 60 million years ago, I said "au revoir" to Africa (then a super-continent known as Gondwana) and sailed off to find myself!

I evolved my very own curiosity cabinet of species, including the spear-nosed snake, the inch-long Brookesia chameleon, 60 species of lemur, and 1000 species of orchids. To explore, tiptoe through my Tsingy rock formations: With sharp shards of eroded limestone and karst, their name means "land where one cannot walk barefoot." Even my Malagasy people are unique: Half the population have genes from Borneo, over 4500 miles (7240 km) away, suggesting that their ancestors arrived due to shipwreck! Speaking of wrecks, in 2015 a sunken ship was discovered just off my shore; the silver treasure found inside suggests it was the ship of the Scottish pirate Captain Kidd.

SIZE: 226,658 sq mi (587,041 sq km)

POPULATION: 24,430,000

CURRENCY: Malagasy ariary

CAPITAL: Antananarivo

LANGUAGES: French, Malagasy

Comoros

AFRICA

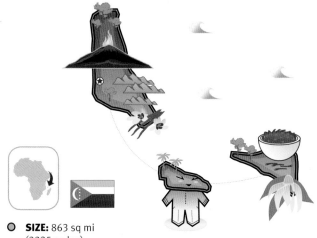

Ka-boom! I'm explosive: Mount Karthala on my Grand Comore island has erupted 20 times in the past 100 years—yet the Karthala scops owl makes these volcanic slopes its home. My people aren't placid either—they've staged 20 coups since gaining independence from France. Chill, guys—try aromatherapy; it's my specialty! I'm known as Perfume Island for my vanilla, clove, and ylang-ylang exports. Chanel No. 5 would be nothing without me!

- **SIZE:** 863 sq mi (2235 sq km)
- **POPULATION:** 795,000
- **CURRENCY:** Comorian franc
- **CAPITAL:** Moroni
- **LANGUAGES:** Arabic, French, Shikomoro

Seychelles

AFRICA

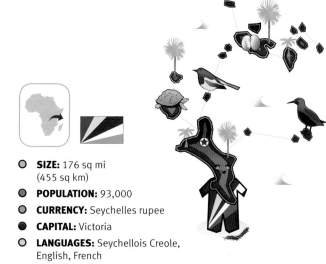

Unusual species live on my Indian Ocean archipelago of 115 granite and coral islands. Take my rare 256-legged giant millipedes—proper janitors that recycle 17 percent of my leaf litter through their guts every 24 hours, making the soil fertile enough to support my coco de mer tree, among others. My Aride Island attracts giant Aldabra tortoises and endangered native birds: the gray sooty noddy and the blue-black magpie robin.

- **SIZE:** 176 sq mi (455 sq km)
- **POPULATION:** 93,000
- **CURRENCY:** Seychelles rupee
- **CAPITAL:** Victoria
- **LANGUAGES:** Seychellois Creole, English, French

Mauritius

* Mauritius has depended on sugar production ever since colonial times
* In the popular folk dance, the *sega*, a dancer's feet never leave the ground

SIZE: 788 sq mi (2040 sq km)

POPULATION: 1,348,000

CURRENCY: Mauritian rupee

CAPITAL: Port Louis

LANGUAGES: English, Creole

A small volcanic island in the Indian Ocean, I form part of the Mascarene Islands 500 miles (800 km) east of Madagascar and am surrounded by coral reefs. My most famous native, the flightless dodo bird, went extinct long ago, leaving me and my mostly Hindu population (descendants of Indian servants imported by past European colonizers) to mind our own business. Among my features are white sand beaches favored by dolphins and the idyllic Chamarel waterfall. Check out my seven colored dunes—red, brown, violet, blue, green, yellow, and purple—formed by iron and aluminum oxides in the sand. Or stroll across my natural stone bridges formed by pounding surf on the rockier side of my coastline.

When scientists analyzed zircon crystals in my cliffs, they deduced that the cliffs were older than the rest of me—much older: I formed just nine million years ago, compared to the almost three-billion-year age of the cliffs. It seems I've been concealing the lost supercontinent of Mauritia all these years!

Asia

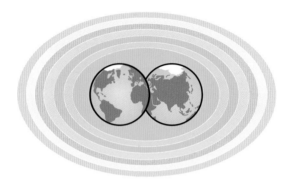

I'm sprawled out on Earth's surface like I own it—well, I am the planet's largest, most populous continent. And although my Tibetan monks may practice the art of silence, when it comes to my history, I'm loud and proud. My Mongolian horsemen were the centaurs of the steppes; their hard riding on tough little ponies helped Genghis Khan create the Mongol Empire, history's largest continuous land empire.

- **Land mass:** 17,212,000 sq mi (44,579,000 sq km)
- **Number of countries:** 47

I'm riding high: My Tibetan plateau, "the roof of the world," is 3 miles (5 km) above sea level and bordered by Everest and K2, the world's two highest mountains. I'm bordered by the Ural Mountains in the west, but my southeastern reaches harbor the most wonderful water worlds. My Badjao people are sea nomads, living on *vintas* (houseboats) and free-diving the deep to harvest pearls and fish.

- **Biggest lake:** Baikal
- **Longest river:** Yangtze
- **Highest mountain:** Everest

135

Asia

 Afghanistan

 Armenia

 Azerbaijan

 Bahrain

 Bangladesh

 Bhutan

 Brunei

 Cambodia

 China, People's Republic of

 East Timor

 Georgia

 India

 Indonesia

 Iran

 Iraq

 Israel

 Japan

 Jordan

 Kazakhstan

 Kuwait

 Kyrgyzstan

 Laos

 Lebanon

 Malaysia

 Maldives

 Mongolia

Myanmar

Nepal

 North Korea

 Oman

 Pakistan

 Philippines

 Qatar

Saudi Arabia

 Singapore

 South Korea

 Sri Lanka

Black Sea

Georgia

Caspian Sea

Uzbekis...

Armenia Azerbaijan

Turkmenis...

Turkey

Syria

Iran

Mediterranean Sea

Lebanon

Iraq

Israel Jordan

Kuwait

Persian Gulf

Bahrain

Qatar

U.A.E.

Red Sea

Saudi Arabia

Oman

Yemen

Kazakhstan

Mongolia

Kyrgyzstan

Tajikistan

Afghanistan

Pakistan

China

North Korea

Sea of Japan

South Korea

Japan

Nepal

Bhutan

East China Sea

India

Myanmar

Bangladesh

Laos

Taiwan

Arabian Sea

Bay of Bengal

Thailand

Vietnam

Pacific Ocean

Cambodia

South China Sea

Philippine Sea

Philippines

Sri Lanka

Maldives

Indian Ocean

Malaysia

Brunei

Singapore

Indonesia

East Timor

Syria

Taiwan

Tajikistan

Thailand

Turkey

Turkmenistan

United Arab Emirates

Uzbekistan

Vietnam

Yemen

Turkey

ASIA

- ✳ Ankara's tallest building, Atakule Tower, offers 360-degree views over the city
- ✳ The impressive ruins of the ancient Greek city of Ephesus stand on the coast of Ionia
- ✳ The Tigris River rises in the Taurus Mountains of eastern Turkey

My irregular shape and strategic location have been useful to my people over the centuries. You see, with three percent of my land in southeastern Europe (that includes my major city, Istanbul) and 97 percent in southwestern Asia, I act as a bridge between the two continents. Not only that, but my Turkish Straits, the Bosporus and Dardanelles, are the ultimate connectors between the Mediterranean and the Black Sea, between Europe, Russia, and Ukraine.

Did you know I'm the site of ancient Troy, where the Greek hero Odysseus duped the Trojans by hiding an army in a massive wooden horse? Or that Mount Ararat, the enormous volcanic mountain on my border with Armenia and Iran, is the spot where Noah is said to have landed his ark?

Care to go for a spin? Check out my whirling dervishes—Islamic holy men who spin in circles to get closer to Allah. Had enough? Go to ground in Cappadocia. My central region hides over 30 underground cities and thousands of churches carved over centuries into the soft basaltic rock. Stop on the way to buy some Turkish Delight; my signature sweetmeat is dried fruits and nuts suspended in a sweet starchy gel.

- ○ **SIZE:** 302,535 sq mi (783,562 sq km)
- ◉ **POPULATION:** 80,275,000
- ◎ **CURRENCY:** Turkish lira
- ● **CAPITAL:** Ankara
- ○ **LANGUAGE:** Turkish

Pamukkale ("Cotton Castle")

A glistening, white landscape of terraces and waterfalls awaits visitors to Pamukkale. The forms result from the buildup of white calcite deposits carried by the local natural warm-water springs.

Holy Architecture

Two sacred buildings stand within sight of one another in Istanbul. The rosy red Hagia Sophia was built as a church in 360 c.e. and converted into a mosque in 1453. It is now a museum. Sultan Ahmed Mosque, known as the Blue Mosque for its interior blue tiles, was built in 1616.

Armenia

ASIA

I may be small, but I am also immensely old. My ancient earth is rich in minerals, notably copper (my main export) from my Kajaran mine, but also gold and even the odd diamond or two. Aboveground, snap some shots of my fortresses—say, at Amberd or Bjni—before making your way to my high-altitude Lake Sevan. During my long, hot summers, locals love to hang out on the lake's beaches, eating crawfish caught in its cool waters.

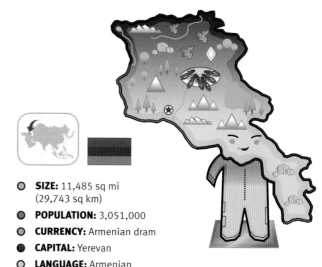

- **SIZE:** 11,485 sq mi (29,743 sq km)
- **POPULATION:** 3,051,000
- **CURRENCY:** Armenian dram
- **CAPITAL:** Yerevan
- **LANGUAGE:** Armenian

Georgia

ASIA

S ay "cheese" ("*qveli*") when you see me, for food is never a problem. Lush with green valleys, my highland terrain stretches east from the Black Sea. *Rtveli*, my September harvest, yields tea, peanuts, and grapes galore. Scenic mountains and ancient architecture ensure superb snapshots, and wildlife is great. Be sure to catch one of my colorful native birds: a pink-breasted great rosefinch or the striking Güldenstädt's redstart.

- **SIZE:** 29, 911 sq mi (69,700 sq km)
- **POPULATION:** 4,928,000
- **CURRENCY:** Georgian lari
- **CAPITAL:** Tbilisi
- **LANGUAGE:** Georgian

Azerbaijan

ASIA

* Azerbaijan's national animal, the Karabakh horse, is one of the world's oldest breeds
* Baku's seafront carpet museum is shaped like a rolled-up rug

○ **SIZE:** 31,903 sq mi (82,629 sq km)

◉ **POPULATION:** 9,873,000

○ **CURRENCY:** Azerbaijani manat

● **CAPITAL:** Baku

○ **LANGUAGE:** Azerbaijani

I'm burning red-hot right now! Freedom from Soviet control (gained in 1991) has fanned my flames of ambition. My oil and gas resources have been famous since medieval times, and today, oil money is fueling some pyrotechnic architecture—just look at my capital Baku's Flame Towers, if you don't believe me. My Baku Ateshgah is a Zoroastrian temple and monastic complex built over a natural gas well; the temple flame is fueled by gas seeps. At Yanar Dag, on my Absheron Peninsula, gas seeping from beneath the bedrock burns permanently in an ever-burning brush fire.

My natural resources love to show off: The strawberry and white swirls of my Candy Cane Mountains (think Christmas ribbon candy) are the result of a chemical reaction between the minerals in the rocks and groundwater.

Syria

ASIA

- ☀ The Umayyad Mosque in the walled city of Damascus is one of the world's oldest
- ☀ Sand-bearing wind blows a wall of dust across the land once or twice a year

Known in ancient days as Sham, I was once famed for my swordsmiths, who honed swirl-patterned Damascus steel blades able to slice through a floating silk scarf, and for the Hurrian Hymn, the world's first melody written in musical notation—a song for the lute. But in 2011, a civil war began that ravaged my land; the sounds that shatter my skies are no longer harmonious.

The Euphrates River runs through my arid landscape—mostly desert plateau rimmed by the Bishri Mountains to the north and the Anti-Lebanon range to the west. I'm short on vegetation—blame my poor soils. You'll find citrus trees in my coastal region, date palms in the Euphrates valley, and hardy evergreens on my mountain slopes. Today, my country bears the scars of air and mortar strikes, but I am no stranger to conflict. My land is scattered with Crusader-era castles, such as the 10th- century Masyaf Castle, secret hideout of the Assassins, a medieval-era Ismaili sect feared for the slaying of its religious enemies!

- ○ **SIZE:** 71,498 sq mi (185,180 sq km)
- ◉ **POPULATION:** 17,185,000
- ○ **CURRENCY:** Syrian pound
- ● **CAPITAL:** Damascus
- ○ **LANGUAGE:** Arabic

Lebanon

ASIA

You won't guess what covers 13 percent of my land . . . cedar trees! They grow up to 130 feet (40 m) tall, and King Solomon used them to build his temple in nearby Jerusalem. People come to ski in my mountains—the name of the oldest and highest resort is Cedars Ski Resort (what else?). When done with the ski runs, head to my cosmopolitan capital by the sea, where you can chill out on the beach or ogle the superyachts moored in the marina.

- ○ **SIZE:** 4015 sq mi (10,400 sq km)
- ◑ **POPULATION:** 6,238,000
- ○ **CURRENCY:** Lebanese pound
- ● **CAPITAL:** Beirut
- ○ **LANGUAGE:** Arabic

Jordan

ASIA

Guides to my ancient rock-carved site of Petra tell people it's "half as old as time." And when a movie includes action on Mars, I tell people it was probably shot in the red-sand desert at Wadi Rum. If you are not a fan of summer heat, my tip is to go float in my oh-so-salty Dead Sea or to snorkel off my teeny 16-mile (26-km) coast on the Gulf of Aqaba. But I don't recommend being baptized in my Jordan River—it's pretty polluted these days.

- ○ **SIZE:** 34,496 sq m. (89,342 sq km)
- ◑ **POPULATION:** 8,185,000
- ○ **CURRENCY:** Jordanian dinar
- ● **CAPITAL:** Amman
- ○ **LANGUAGE:** Arabic

Israel

ASIA

☀ Archaeologists have unearthed a 2500-year-old dog cemetery at Ashkelon
☀ The Mount Carmel mountain range to the north is Israel's largest national park

Scout my territory, and you'll encounter sites sacred to Judaism, Christianity, and Islam. On Jerusalem's Temple Mount are the Dome of the Rock, the traditional site where Muhammad made his night journey to Paradise (Islam) and where Abraham led Isaac to sacrifice (Judaism); the Stone of Unction, where Jesus's body was prepared for burial (Christianity); and the Western "Wailing" Wall, Judaism's holiest site. My sparsely settled southern Negev desert is home to *makhtesh*, deep canyons ground out by erosion that display evidence of my prehistoric past in colorful rock strata. The springs there attract ibex and Arabian leopards. The Jordan River runs south from my northern hills of Galilee to form my border with Jordan.

My territory may be ancient, but as a country I'm not even 100 years old. My creation as a homeland for Jews in 1948 displaced native Palestinians. I continue to occupy Palestinian land, such as the West Bank, and this has caused decades of bitter fighting.

- **SIZE:** 8,019 sq mi (20,770 sq km)
- **POPULATION:** 8,175,000
- **CURRENCY:** Israeli new shekel
- **CAPITAL:** Tel Aviv-Yafo
- **LANGUAGES:** Hebrew, Arabic

Saudi Arabia

ASIA

* Saudi's nomadic Bedouins are known for sword dancing and hunting with falcons
* King Fahd's Fountain, in the city of Jeddah, is the tallest fountain in the world

Occupying most of the Arabian Peninsula, my territory includes three major deserts: the Rub' al Khali, An Nafud, and ad-Dahna—the world's largest sand-only desert expanses. The Rub' al Khali, known as the "Empty Quarter," is uninhabited—but it is crossed by miles of oil pipelines.

No rivers cross my terrain. So? I'm a shipping powerhouse, thanks to coastlines on both the Persian Gulf and the Red Sea. And don't forget my "desert ships"— charismatic Arabian camels that can store up to 80 pounds (36 kg) of fat in their humps. Plus, there's something more precious flowing beneath me: only 265 billion barrels or so of oil! I also sit on caves: My Umm er Radhuma rock bed is pocked with limestone caverns, including a deep one known as the Father of Fear! My people drink thick coffee flavored with ginger and cardamom. Many of them also practice an austere form of Islam known as Wahhabism, which interprets the words of the Islamic text, the Koran, strictly.

SIZE: 830,000 sq mi (2,149,690 sq km)

POPULATION: 28,160,000

CURRENCY: Saudi riyal

CAPITAL: Riyadh

LANGUAGE: Arabic

Oman

ASIA

Come and explore my desert, camping out under the stars at night. The beautiful red and brown dunes at A'Sharqiyah Sands stretch over 38,000 square miles (98,420 sq km). This is Bedouin territory—take a camel ride to get a feel for the nomadic life, or speed across the sand in a dune buggy. Later, cool off in the shade at my Bahla fort, or chill on the beach at Muscat. You might spot a dolphin or two, if you're lucky.

- **SIZE:** 119,499 sq mi (309,500 sq km)
- **POPULATION:** 3,355,000
- **CURRENCY:** Oman rial
- **CAPITAL:** Muscat
- **LANGUAGE:** Arabic

Yemen

ASIA

Mud sticks—it needs to, since my most attractive feature is my mud-brick architecture: square slabs that can rise several stories high. You can see them in my capital Sana'a and at Wadi Hadhramaut skirting the edge of the Rub' al Khali desert (which I share with Saudi Arabia, Oman, and the U.A.E). My people drink tea and coffee; my Red Sea port of Mocha was once known for exporting coffee to Europe. My honey is famous, too.

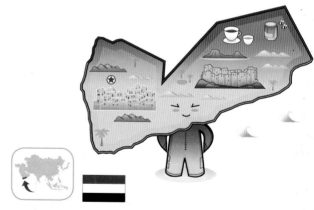

- **SIZE:** 203,850 sq mi (527,968 sq km)
- **POPULATION:** 27,393,000
- **CURRENCY:** Yemeni rial
- **CAPITAL:** Sana'a
- **LANGUAGE:** Arabic

Iran
ASIA

☀ Legend says a three-headed dragon lurks at Mount Damavand, Asia's highest volcano

☀ The Iranians built Tehran's Azadi Tower in celebration of the Persian Empire

Don't be fooled by the plain black robes of my contemporary clerics. At heart, I revel in pattern and color: I'm opulent, like my famed Persian carpets. Even my landscape is rich; it's rimmed by the Zagros and Alborz mountain ranges on two sides and opens to the Caspian Sea in my north and the Persian Gulf and Arabian Sea to the south, where I grow forests of wild pistachio trees. Then there is Qeshm Island off my southern coast, with its mangroves, coral reefs, and Persian melons. Yes, even my food is sumptuous—pomegranates full of ruby-red seeds and my rose-water ice cream—a specialty!

My Safavid dynasty patronized artisans who created velvet and silk textiles featuring people and exotic illustrated manuscripts, such as the 15th-century *Mantiq-al-tayr* (Language of the Birds). In my Isfahan region, the birds live in castles: My people built brick and limestone dovecotes—little towers for doves tunneled with nesting niches; the dung was collected to fertilize fields and tan my famous leather.

SIZE: 636,372 sq mi (1,648,195 sq km)

POPULATION: 82,802,000

CURRENCY: Iranian rial

CAPITAL: Tehran

LANGUAGE: Persian

Iraq

ASIA

- ☀ An ancient ziggurat (a stepped stone pyramid topped by a shrine) stands in the city of Ur
- ☀ Iraq is the world's fourth-largest producer of oil

Assyria, Sumeria, Babylonia, ah, the musical names of my ancient grandeur! Gaze at the *lamassu*, stern stone guardians at the gates of my Assyrian citadels. Winged bulls with the wise heads of warrior kings symbolize the fierce pride that sustains me today, while troubled by violence and unrest.

I was once known as Mesopotamia, or the land between two rivers. The Tigris and Euphrates rivers meander in parallel down my length, then join in my southern town, Al-Qurnah; tradition says their meeting point was the location of the Garden of Eden. The plains around the rivers formed the "fertile crescent," where agriculture nourished one of the earliest civilizations. Head west from here and you'll stray into desert territory. To my south are marshlands, where my Marsh Arab people built huts of reeds and fished. Drained by order of my former ruler, Saddam Hussein, today the wetlands are being restored, attracting birds that include the sacred ibis and Mesopotamian crow.

- **SIZE:** 169,235 sq mi (438,317 sq km)
- **POPULATION:** 38,146,000
- **CURRENCY:** Iraqi dinar
- **CAPITAL:** Baghdad
- **LANGUAGES:** Arabic, Kurdish

Kuwait

ASIA

Apart from my oasis at Al Jahra and a cluster of islands, my land is mostly desert. No wonder my people are seafaring folk. My marinas are full of boats, and who wouldn't want to go sailing or scuba diving in my warm waters? One of the world's smallest countries, I am blessed with oil wells that bring me wealth. I also pack a punch when it comes to architecture—just look at Al Hamra Tower in Kuwait City, or my groovy "mushroom" water towers.

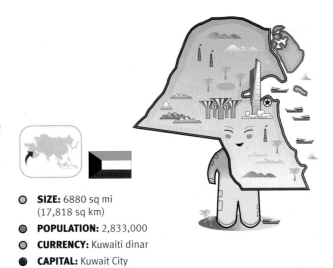

- **SIZE:** 6880 sq mi (17,818 sq km)
- **POPULATION:** 2,833,000
- **CURRENCY:** Kuwaiti dinar
- **CAPITAL:** Kuwait City
- **LANGUAGE:** Arabic

Bahrain

ASIA

Even if you amount to just one small island, you can always expand! Take my Petal Beach resort and the Amwaj Islands in the shallow seas around me—all artificial! Just zip from my mainland on Avenue 59 to check out my Floating City. Many of my residents are from abroad, and plenty come for the motor racing at the Bahrain International Circuit. If cars are not your thing, take a desert safari or head to my Royal Camel Farm at Manama.

- **SIZE:** 293 sq mi (760 sq km)
- **POPULATION:** 1,379,000
- **CURRENCY:** Bahraini dinar
- **CAPITAL:** Manama
- **LANGUAGE:** Arabic

Qatar

ASIA

Trading pearls used to be my specialty, but people mostly talk about my oil these days. And why not? It has made me rich, after all. Just take a look at my skyscraper skyline in Doha—best appreciated from a Persian Gulf cruise on a traditional wooden *dhow*. Or you might just prefer to go shopping in my centuries-old Souq Waqif or visit I. M. Pei's spectacular Museum of Islamic Art on its own specially created island.

- **SIZE:** 4473 sq mi (11,586 sq km)
- **POPULATION:** 2,258,000
- **CURRENCY:** Qatari riyal
- **CAPITAL:** Doha
- **LANGUAGE:** Arabic

United Arab Emirates

ASIA

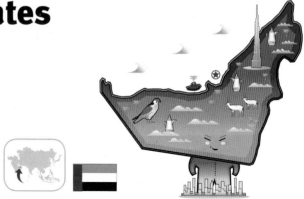

Marhaba—Welcome! A federation of seven emirates that include Abu Dhabi and Dubai, my land is dotted with sculptures of the *dallah*, an Arabic coffee pot, as a mark of my hospitality. You may also spot the odd peregrine falcon—my people love falconry—or the handsome Arabian oryx, my national animal. The world's tallest structure, the Burj Khalifa, stands in Dubai, overlooking amazing (artificial) palm-shaped islands.

- **SIZE:** 32,278 sq mi (83,600 sq km)
- **POPULATION:** 5,927,000
- **CURRENCY:** Emirati dirham
- **CAPITAL:** Abu Dhabi
- **LANGUAGE:** Arabic

Kazakhstan

ASIA

- Astana's skyscrapers include the 490-foot- (150-m-) tall observation Bayterek Tower
- Ibex and mountain sheep roam Aksu-Zhabagly nature reserve

- **SIZE:** 1,052,090 sq mi (2,724,900 sq km)
- **POPULATION:** 18,360,000
- **CURRENCY:** Kazakh tenge
- **CAPITAL:** Astana
- **LANGUAGES:** Kazakh, Russian

The world's largest landlocked country, I stretch my expanse of grass, shrubland, and mountains across two continents, from Europe to Asia. Horsemen once rode galloping steeds across my steppes and my people still feel at home on horseback to this day. Put it down to a history of nomadic mobility—Kazakhstan means "land of the wanderers"—and the fact that horse sausage and fermented mare's milk are delicacies here!

Would you believe that *Malus sieversii*, one of the apple's key ancestors, grows in my Altai Mountains? And that wild tulips are native to my steppes?

Modern Kazakhs live in cities such as Astana, and enjoy a booming economy created by my oil and mineral wealth. They can marvel at the Khan Shatyr, a modernistic mall that looks like a traditional Kazakh yurt (tent).

Uzbekistan

ASIA

Dry and crusty, that's me! My deserts and mountains are landlocked, and my rivers never reach the sea. But, with four good seasons a year, wildlife thrives in my forests and green valleys; you might just be lucky enough to spot a snow leopard or brown bear. My ancient cities of Bukhara and Samarkand—once stopping places on the old Silk Route from China—are still known for making rugs and fine embroidery.

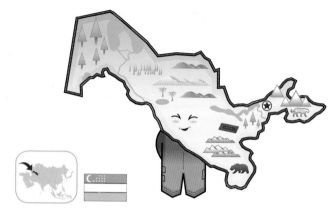

- **SIZE:** 172,742 sq mi (447,400 sq km)
- **POPULATION:** 29,474,000
- **CURRENCY:** Uzbekistani so'm
- **CAPITAL:** Tashkent
- **LANGUAGE:** Uzbek

Turkmenistan

ASIA

The Amu River flows through my northeast; to the south lie mountains. In between, crossed by camels, my vast deserts are so full of gas and oil that I can supply energy to my neighbors. The Silk Road once passed through my territory—you'll see the ruins of Merv, once considered the largest metropolis in the world—so it is not surprising that my national costumes, embroidered with birds and flowers, are often made of silk.

- **SIZE:** 188,456 sq mi (488,100 sq km)
- **POPULATION:** 5,291,000
- **CURRENCY:** Turkmen manat
- **CAPITAL:** Ashgabat
- **LANGUAGE:** Turkmen

Kyrgyzstan
ASIA

❋ The world's largest wild walnut forest grows in the Jalal-Abad region of Kyrgyzstan

❋ The agile snow leopard thrives in the rugged, sparsely populated terrain

○ **SIZE:** 77,202 sq mi
(199,951 sq km)

◉ **POPULATION:**
5,728,000

○ **CURRENCY:**
Kyrgyzstani som

● **CAPITAL:**
Bishkek

○ **LANGUAGE:**
Kyrgyz

Eighty percent of my land is covered by the Tian Shan mountain range: longer, wider, and nearly as high as the Himalayas. Home is packable here: My nomadic tribes shelter in yurts—circular felt tents fixed to a wooden lattice with braids of horse, yak, or camel hair. The nomads team with fearsomely taloned golden eagles to hunt from horseback! For road food, they pack *kurut*—yak milk that is boiled, then sun-dried to make hard cakes.

Traditional fashions are cozy in winter: coats of sheepskin or wolf fur, *ak kalpaks*—peaked, embroidered white felt hats—for the guys, and *elecheks*, muslin turbans wrapped with embroidered scarves for married women.

Located near Lake Issyk-Kul, my Kumtor gold mine was once a stopover on the Silk Road caravan route. Battle-axes and a gold bar have been found at the bottom of the lake.

Tajikistan

ASIA

* Tajikistan's many mountains are home to brown bears, goats, and golden eagles
* Soviet-era canals help irrigate cotton plantations and vineyards

○ **SIZE:** 55,637 sq mi
(144,100 sq km)

○ **POPULATION:**
8,331,000

○ **CURRENCY:**
Tajikistani somoni

● **CAPITAL:**
Dushanbe

○ **LANGUAGES:**
Tajik, Russian

Hidden deep in Muslim Asia, I'm crammed to my borders with mountains: At least 50 percent of my land is more than 9800 feet (3000 m) up—I hope you have a head for heights! Lakes and rivers riddle my territory and I am sure it will surprise you to learn that I possess the world's largest nonpolar glacier. If you're looking for agriculture, try Fergana Valley in my north. You'll find mostly cotton, but also fruits, grains, and vegetables.

My Marco Polo sheep, named after the 13th-century explorer who first described them, weigh up to 400 pounds (181 kg) and sport magnificent spiraling horns. Perched high in my Pamir Mountains, my Kuh-i-Lal mine has been in business since 7 C.E. At that time it was known for rare, golden clinohumite—red-gold nuggets, like my famously sweet apricots: impossibly juicy jewels from the ancient orchards of my Isfara region.

Afghanistan

ASIA

* Afghanistan's mosques include the 15th-century Shrine of Ali in Mazar-i-Sharif
* *Ashak* is a popular dish of leek-stuffed ravioli, topped with minced meat and yogurt

- **SIZE:** 251,827 sq mi (652,230 sq km)
- **POPULATION:** 33,332,000
- **CURRENCY:** Afghan afghani
- **CAPITAL:** Kabul
- **LANGUAGES:** Afghan Persian (Dari), Pashto

No stranger to conflict, I have suffered war and political instability for decades. My territory is shaky, too—just look at my fearsome Hindu Kush mountains. Due to the underthrust of the Indian tectonic plate beneath the Eurasian plate, this is one of the most earthquake-prone zones on Earth. Running through the mountains, the Khyber Pass connects my land with Pakistan. It's been a strategic military route for centuries.

Today I may seem a monotone moonscape of somber tan, but my past is glittered with gold. My location at a crossroads of Silk Road trade routes between China, India, and the Mediterranean meant that I once bustled as a commercial hub. In Tillya Tepe, west of Mazar-i-Sharif, an excavated earthen burial mound revealed a tribal prince buried with his horse, five wives, and more than 20,000 pieces of gold and precious stone jewelry.

India
ASIA

* ❋ Emperor Shah Jahan built the Taj Mahal—a marble mausoleum—in memory of his wife
* ❋ India is the world's largest producer of mangoes; Indians eat the most mangoes, too
* ❋ Blackbucks—black-blanketed antelopes with spiraled horns—roam the Thar Desert

Sparse is not my style. Consider my saris, jewelry, temples, and food: I'm embroidered, brocaded, appliquéd, embellished, enameled, encrusted, inlaid, studded, and highly spiced. Yup, I'm one truly ornate country! Even my outline is diamond-shaped, crowned by the perilous peaks of the Himalayas to my north and engraved by the Ganges and Indus Rivers carving out the fertile Ganges River Valley to my south. The Sundarbans, the world's largest mangrove forest, coil their twisted tangle of roots around my Bay of Bengal border with Bangladesh; flame-striped Bengal tigers wade through their swamps.

In my city of Madurai, 33,000 carved stone sculptures of animals, gods, and demons adorn my Meenakshi Amman Temple, painted in rainbow hues; green parrots trained to caw "*Meenakshi*," the name of the temple goddess, squawk at the entrance to the interior sanctuary.

I even celebrate new growth in technicolor—at Holi, a holiday that follows spring's first full moon. My whole land becomes a rampaging mass of people throwing paint and pigment in the air, until all are covered in indigo blue, rose madder red, herbal green, and marigold yellow powdered dyes.

- ⊙ **SIZE:** 1,269,219 sq mi (3,287,263 sq km)
- ◉ **POPULATION:** 1,266,884,000
- ◉ **CURRENCY:** Indian rupee
- ● **CAPITAL:** New Delhi
- ⊙ **LANGUAGES:** Hindi, Bengali, Telugu, Marathi, Tamil, Urdu, Gujarati, Malayalam, Kannada, Oriya, Punjabi, Assamese, Kashmiri, Sindhi, Sanskrit

River Rituals

Varanasi, an ancient city on the banks of the Ganges River, is holy to Hindus. Daily morning and evening religious rituals take place on the stepped stone embankments that reach down to the water's edge.

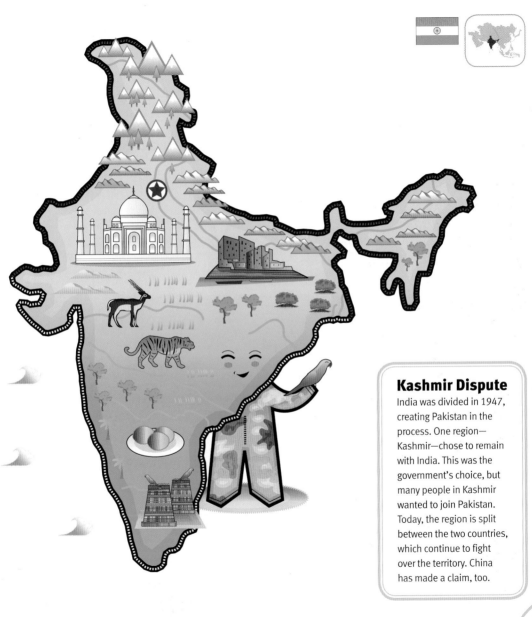

Kashmir Dispute

India was divided in 1947, creating Pakistan in the process. One region—Kashmir—chose to remain with India. This was the government's choice, but many people in Kashmir wanted to join Pakistan. Today, the region is split between the two countries, which continue to fight over the territory. China has made a claim, too.

Pakistan

ASIA

❋ The name Pakistan means "Land of the Pure"

❋ Lahore's Minar-e-Pakistan monument towers 230 feet (70 m) above Iqbal Park

I'm a very new country, created in 1947 to be a Muslim homeland after the British left India and the country was divided. To my north loom the Karakoram Mountains, including deadly K2, the world's most dangerous mountain. The Indus River flows along my entire length from north to south and empties into the Arabian Sea near Karachi; the valley around the river was the site of a highly developed farming civilization in 2500 B.C.E., known for its carved tablets representing animals and for carnelian ornaments. Shah Jahan, the greatest of the Mughal Empire emperors, who directed the creation of the Taj Mahal in India, was born in my city Lahore in 1592.

Traveling my Karakoram Highway—the world's highest paved road—from Abbottabad to Kashgar in China can get a little dicey. (Think landslides, snow avalanches, the Khunjerab Pass at 15,397 feet/4693 m above sea level.) My people decorate their trucks with evil-eye motifs, turning them into mobile lucky charms.

○ **SIZE:** 307,374 sq mi (796,095 sq km)

● **POPULATION:** 201,996,000

○ **CURRENCY:** Pakistani rupee

● **CAPITAL:** Islamabad

○ **LANGUAGES:** Urdu, English, Punjabi

Nepal

ASIA

My stand-out feature is the world's tallest mountain, Everest, 29,029 feet (8848 m) above sea level; only 500 climbers reach the peak each year. Others trek the Himalayas and raft down my spectacular white waters. The streets in my old city of Kathmandu lead to ancient wooden buildings, palaces, and temples, such as Boudhanath Stupa, that have survived earthquakes. In Bhaktapur stands the tallest pagoda temple in the country.

- **SIZE:** 56,827 sq mi (147,181 sq km)
- **POPULATION:** 29,034,000
- **CURRENCY:** Nepalese rupee
- **CAPITAL:** Kathmandu
- **LANGUAGE:** Nepali

Bhutan

ASIA

A small kingdom high in the Himalayas, I'm admired for my beautiful, remote Buddhist monasteries and fortresses (*dzong*). I ask outsiders to pay around $250 a day to visit; it covers their costs while controlling tourism. More than 60 percent of my land is protected forest, and my subtropical plains produce my unique red rice. The takin, a goat-antelope, is my national animal, and I have black bears and red pandas, too.

- **SIZE:** 14,824 sq mi (38,394 sq km)
- **POPULATION:** 750,000
- **CURRENCY:** Bhutanese ngultrum
- **CAPITAL:** Thimphu
- **LANGUAGES:** Dzongkha, Sharchhopka

Bangladesh

ASIA

My three big rivers, the Ganges, the Brahmaputra, and the Meghna, tend to flood, so my resourceful people build homes that are easy to move and farm shrimp and crab for export. My city Dhaka has become a center of the garment trade. I also produce paper, using pulp made from bamboo that grows in my Chittagong Hills. In my cities, you'll see people using cycle rickshaws. In the countryside, look for clouded leopards.

- **SIZE:** 57,320 sq mi (148,460 sq km)
- **POPULATION:** 156,187,000
- **CURRENCY:** Bangladeshi taka
- **CAPITAL:** Dhaka
- **LANGUAGE:** Bengali

Sri Lanka

ASIA

Ooh, I love a cup of tea, which is fortunate because my hillsides are covered in plantations that produce Ceylon tea (Ceylon's my old name). To eat, I like fishy coconut curries. That's lucky, too, because I am surrounded by the sea and coconuts grow here in their thousands. In my forests—of mahogany, ebony, and teak—elephants help by lifting trunks with their trunks! You can see hundreds of them in the wild at my Uda Walawe National Park.

- **SIZE:** 25,332 sq mi (65,610 sq km)
- **POPULATION:** 22,235,000
- **CURRENCY:** Sri Lankan rupee
- **CAPITAL:** Sri Jayawardenepura Kotte
- **LANGUAGES:** Sinhala, Tamil

Maldives

ASIA

I am the smallest Asian country, with dozens of atolls and islands scattered across the Indian Ocean. Getting around on a traditional *dhoni* boat is fun—except in the monsoon season. Many visitors come to dive in my sapphire-blue waters, to see the colorful coral and beautiful fish, such as the butterflyfish and angelfish. My cowrie (sea-snail) shells were once used as a currency, and you will see them as a symbol on our national bank bills.

- **SIZE:** 115 sq mi (298 sq km)
- **POPULATION:** 393,000
- **CURRENCY:** Maldivian rufiyaa
- **CAPITAL:** Malé
- **LANGUAGE:** Bahasa Malaysia

Taiwan

ASIA

I'm a techno-whizz—computers are my thing. My cities are mostly coastal: Ancient Tainan lies to my west and Taipei, with its famous tower, to my north. Mountains dominate my eastern territory, peaking with mighty Yushan. Rice grows on lower slopes, all lush and green in summer. In July, the Taitung festival fills my sky with hot-air balloons of all colors. Politically, China sees me as a rebel that it wants to control, but I'd rather be independent.

- **SIZE:** 52,502 sq m (35,980 sq km)
- **POPULATION:** 23,465,000
- **CURRENCY:** New Taiwan Dollar
- **CAPITAL:** Taipei
- **LANGUAGE:** Mandarin Chinese

People's Republic of China

ASIA

- Ancient wonders include the Great Wall of China and an 8000-strong Terra-Cotta Army
- A popular motif, the Chinese dragon features in traditional dances and ceremonies
- Hong Kong's skyline has more skyscrapers than any other city in the world

Foreheads to the floor: You may kowtow to me! As the imperial home of the savvy sages who invented gunpowder, the mariner's compass, and printing, I think I've earned a few humble bows! I give my name to the finest porcelain, and the plant that helps us all carry on—*Camellia sinensis* (that's tea to you)—was first cultivated here. I'm mad for mulberries: White mulberries feed my silkworms, and in 105 C.E., I pressed the world's first paper from chopped mulberry bark and hemp rags.

Efforts to preserve the panda's habitat in my misty, bamboo-forested Minshan and Qinling Mountains mean the crucial watersheds that flow into my Yangtze and Yellow rivers are also saved. Other inhabitants of these remote cloud forests are protected, too—the takin ox, tree-dwelling red pandas, and Chinese golden pheasants. The city of Turpan, once an oasis on my Silk Road, is rimmed by the Flaming Mountains, red sandstone peaks, the erosion of which has left them looking like flames.

Nine of my cities qualify as megacities, each with more than ten million inhabitants: You can scale skyscrapers in Guangdong and Shanghai and cross numerous bridges in Chongqing. In Beijing's Forbidden City palace complex, take your pick of no fewer than 9000 rooms.

- **SIZE:** 3,705,407 sq mi (9,596,960 sq km)
- **POPULATION:** 1,373,541,000
- **CURRENCY:** Chinese renminbi
- **CAPITAL:** Beijing
- **LANGUAGE:** Chinese

Silken Secrets

China's signature fabric is silk. The secret of its manufacture from a protein in silkworm cocoons was discovered in around 2700 B.C.E. The penalty for revealing the secret to the outside world was death!

Territorial Disputes

Several regions within the PRC, including Tibet and Uighur, are autonomous—they govern themselves. Hong Kong and Macau are cities with special administrative status. This means these places govern themselves to some extent, but are not independent from China.

South Korea

ASIA

- ☀ South Koreans make more than 100 types of *kimchi*—a dish of fermented vegetables
- ☀ Automobiles and cell phones are among South Korea's main exports

Occupying the southern end of the Korean Peninsula, I have three coasts. Between them, green rolling hills and mountains dominate my land. In the olden days, my cross-country communications were sent by *bongsu*—torchlight and smoke signals. The beacon mound on my Namsan Mountain is just one of many strategic signaling spots. Today, I prefer to communicate via the Internet, and the message is crystal clear: I am the "It" country of the 21st century.

K-Culture is exploding: K-pop fangirls dance their way in sync across the Asian continent and Seoul's Coex Center is home to Asia's biggest underground shopping mall. Fortress remnants at Seoul and Hwaseong may testify to my ancient history, but I'm high-tech at heart. Almost half my population lives in and around my capital, and even those inhabiting my traditional wooden *hanok* (houses) have wifi. It's hardly surprising, since my Internet is the fastest in the world.

- ◯ **SIZE:** 38,502 sq mi (99,720 sq km)
- ◯ **POPULATION:** 50,924,000
- ◯ **CURRENCY:** South Korean won
- ● **CAPITAL:** Seoul
- ◯ **LANGUAGE:** Korean

North Korea

ASIA

With two coasts, one on each side of the Korean Peninsula, I have access to plenty of seafood—mollusks and seaweed are specialties. And I am loaded with iron and coal deposits. My 670 c.e. P'yohun-sa Buddhist temple on Mount Kumgang is one of nearly 200 national treasures. But I have a dark side: My extreme government has keen interest in developing nuclear weapons, while many of my people live in extreme poverty.

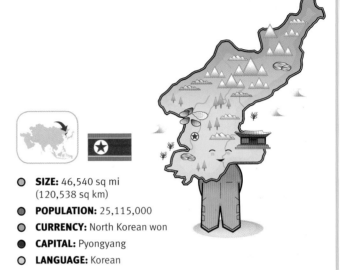

- ○ **SIZE:** 46,540 sq mi (120,538 sq km)
- ◐ **POPULATION:** 25,115,000
- ○ **CURRENCY:** North Korean won
- ● **CAPITAL:** Pyongyang
- ○ **LANGUAGE:** Korean

Mongolia

ASIA

My land is mostly grassland plateau rimmed by mountains and desert. Colliding winds in my Badain Jaran desert create dual-horned barchan sand dunes! To keep the desert at bay, my yurt-dwelling nomadic herders plant native salt cedars and Siberian elm trees. I'm the fabled home of cashmere goats and the Mohawk-maned takhi, the world's only truly wild horse. My native music is played on a horsehead fiddle and features throat singing.

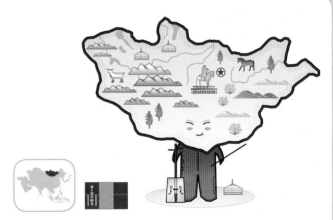

- ○ **SIZE:** 603,909 sq mi (1,564,116 sq km)
- ◐ **POPULATION:** 3,031,000
- ○ **CURRENCY:** Mongolian tögrög
- ● **CAPITAL:** Ulaanbaatar
- ○ **LANGUAGE:** Mongolian

Japan
ASIA

- ✳ At 12,388 feet (3776 m), the dormant volcano of Mount Fuji is Japan's highest mountain
- ✳ Kyoto's Kinkaku-ji temple (the Golden Pavilion) is coated in gold leaf
- ✳ The Shinkansen bullet train reaches speeds of 200 miles per hour (320 km/h)

An archipelago, I comprise four main islands and nearly 6800 islets. Separated from the Asian mainland by more than 120 miles (190 km), I'm a tight-knit family unit: Until recently, more than 98 percent of my people were of "pure" Japanese heritage.

Although my terrain is a challenge to farm, I've mastered the art: For centuries, my mountain slopes have been shaped into graceful terraces that produce abundant rice in little space. Contemporary life relies less on agriculture, though: The urban sprawl of Tokyo, my capital since 1868, is home to around 31 million people.

Tokyo's Shibuya Crossing is said to be the world's most perfectly choreographed intersection, packed with pedestrians moving in sync, like a flock of swallows.

Pickled octopus, anyone? The sea and its bounty are a way of life here: I have one of the world's largest fishing fleets and my people consume more than one-tenth of the world's seafood. The Ama of Shima Peninsula are female free-divers who plunge under the waves to forage for shellfish. My traditional diet of rice, fish, and pickled vegetables means my people live longer: I have a high percentage of centenarians.

- ○ **SIZE:** 145,914 sq mi (377,915 sq km)
- ◉ **POPULATION:** 126,702,000
- ○ **CURRENCY:** Japanese yen
- ● **CAPITAL:** Tokyo
- ○ **LANGUAGE:** Japanese

Ancient Ceremonies

When Japanese people get interested in a subject, they take it to the max! Writing poetry, drinking tea, and even burning incense all have elaborate rituals and implements surrounding their practice.

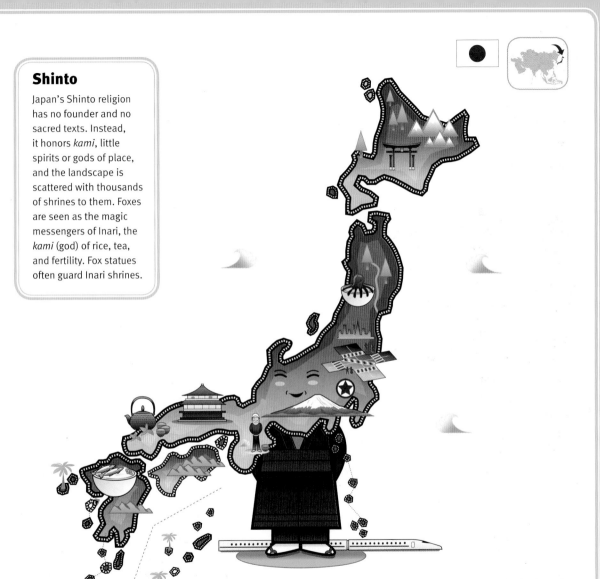

Shinto

Japan's Shinto religion has no founder and no sacred texts. Instead, it honors *kami*, little spirits or gods of place, and the landscape is scattered with thousands of shrines to them. Foxes are seen as the magic messengers of Inari, the *kami* (god) of rice, tea, and fertility. Fox statues often guard Inari shrines.

Myanmar

ASIA

A country with a colorful past, my former royal capital occupies a moated fortress in Mandalay; Yangon is full of golden pagodas and old colonial buildings; and Buddhists in saffron-yellow robes can be seen everywhere, especially at popular pagoda festivals. Tigers roam rain forests dense with hardwoods and fruit trees. My southern delta wetlands are home to turtle and crocodile sanctuaries, and great flocks of migrating birds.

- **SIZE:** 261,228 sq mi (676,578 sq km)
- **POPULATION:** 56,890,000
- **CURRENCY:** Myanmar kyat
- **CAPITAL:** Rangoon
- **LANGUAGE:** Burmese

Laos

ASIA

L uring travelers a-plenty, mine is a dramatic landscape of limestone cliffs and rivers. Abundant rain keeps my rice fields and tea plantations looking lush. I have no coast, but Vientiane, my "city of sandalwood," is on the Mekong River; people gather here to watch spectacular sunsets and enjoy the night market with bowls of *klao niaw* (sticky rice). Pha That Luang, the city's golden Buddhist stupa, has become a national emblem.

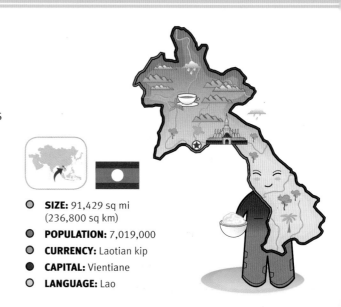

- **SIZE:** 91,429 sq mi (236,800 sq km)
- **POPULATION:** 7,019,000
- **CURRENCY:** Laotian kip
- **CAPITAL:** Vientiane
- **LANGUAGE:** Lao

Cambodia

ASIA

- ☀ Biannual monsoons bring more than three-quarters of the country's annual rainfall
- ☀ Cambodians eat plenty of fish—fresh, dried, smoked, and salted

- **SIZE:** 69,898 sq mi (181,035 sq km)
- **POPULATION:** 15,957,000
- **CURRENCY:** Cambodian riel
- **CAPITAL:** Phnom Penh
- **LANGUAGE:** Khmer

Sure, the massive twining roots of kapok and strangler fig trees sprouting from my temple ruins at Ta Prohm are impressive. But my real religious gem is Angkor Wat, the monumental temple complex founded by Suryavarman II in the 12th century in honor of the Hindu god Vishnu. Three thousand *apsaras* (sacred nymphs) adorn its gateways. Their stories feature in the choreography of my Cambodian classical dancers.

The Mekong River flows south through my eastern region and much of my land is forested. My rosewood and resin trees are at risk, though: Their wood is valuable, and my deforestation rate is one of the world's highest. My southwestern Cardamom Mountains, named for their wild-growing spice, are home to elephants, gaur (wild cattle), Siamese crocodiles, and pileated gibbons. Take care to avoid the cobras!

Thailand

ASIA

- More than 40,000 Buddhist temples dot the Thai landscape
- The native blind cavefish can shimmy its way straight up waterfalls

With gibbons cartwheeling through my teak treetops, a tradition of wandering forest monks, and a beach party in full swing on my southern island of Phuket, I'd say the only resident getting a rest here is my massive reclining gold Buddha. Tradition says my Emerald Buddha (actually sculpted from jade) was revealed when lightning struck a Chiang Mai temple in the 15th century.

My diverse species are losing ground due to habitat loss, but what marvels they are! When my golden-necklaced sunbear unfurls his 10-inch- (25-cm-) long tongue, it's mop-up time for termites and my clouded leopards are known for their now-you-see-them-now-you-don't presence in my deepest rain forest, said to be the world's oldest. My people are pistol-packing—water pistols, that is. During Songkran, my New Year festival, people wash away the past year's sins in a three-day-long water fight. To float away bad luck and honor the river goddess, they send candle-laden banana-leaf boats sailing down rivers.

○ **SIZE:** 198,117 sq mi (513,120 sq km)

◉ **POPULATION:** 68,201,000

◎ **CURRENCY:** Thai baht

● **CAPITAL:** Bangkok

○ **LANGUAGE:** Thai

Vietnam
ASIA

☀ Hang Son Doong Cave, the largest in the world, has its own river, jungle, and climate
☀ Vietnam is the world's largest exporter of black pepper and cashew nuts

SIZE: 127,881 sq mi (331,210 sq km)

POPULATION: 95,261,000

CURRENCY: Vietnamese dong

CAPITAL: Hanoi

LANGUAGE: Vietnamese

I'm a dreamy waterworld, shimmery and reflective. The beaches of my 2025-mile (3260-km) coastline are a tourist draw, but it's on the rivers, canals, and flooded fields of my Mekong River delta that daily life flows. No parking lots here: Even the markets are afloat, with narrow, lantern-hung boats piled high with local fish and fruits. Agricultural produce can be seen gracing household altars, where it joins other ritual items—joss sticks (incense), candles, and photos of deceased ancestors.

Even my puppet shows are waterborne: "Making puppets dance on water" is a tradition dating back to the 11th century. Water buffaloes, my iconic animal, used to plow fields and pull carts, are often tended by children. In Hanoi, Hoan Kiem Lake is the murky realm of Cua Rua (Grandfather), my sacred giant turtle. Near Fansipan, my highest mountain, Sapa rice terraces hand carved a thousand years ago are still tended by the Hmong, one of my hill tribes.

Malaysia

ASIA

* Malaysia's two regions are separated by 640 miles (1030 km) of South China Sea
* *Nasi lemak*—coconut-milk-infused rice—is often served wrapped in a banana leaf

- **SIZE:** 127,355 sq mi (329,847 sq km)
- **POPULATION:** 30,950,000
- **CURRENCY:** Malaysian ringgit
- **CAPITAL:** Kuala Lumpur
- **LANGUAGE:** Bahasa Malaysia

Occupying both the Malay peninsula and the northern half of the island of Borneo, I like to spread myself out. I police the Malacca Strait, vital to shipping lanes linking the Indian and Pacific Oceans. Once a tiny tin-mining town, now my city Kuala Lumpur is a futuristic fantasia: The pedestrian bridge spanning the space between its twin Petronas Towers is 558 feet (170 m) off the ground!

Edible nests cemented with bird spit are harvested from my vaulted Gomantong Caves. Prized for Chinese bird's nest soup, they fetch up to $2000 per kilo. I'm also home to the durian, the fruit with a shell like a spiny grenade and a smelly custard center, and to betel nuts, a traditional gift to Malay brides on their wedding day. My main man of the forests, the orangutan, is humans' closest primate relative.

Philippines
ASIA

* Only one-third of the Philippines' 7000-plus islands are inhabited
* The endangered, 3-foot- (1-m-) tall Philippine eagle is the country's national bird

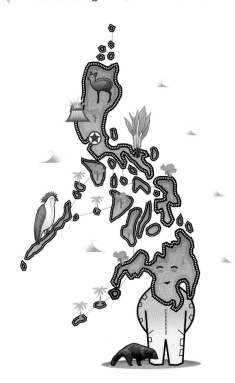

Between them, my mostly mountainous islands boast miles and miles of sandy coastline. But watch out—located on the Pacific's volcano-prone Ring of Fire, I'm a bit of a drama queen. In 1991, I gave in to a major meltdown, kicking up my cranky heels with the 20th-century's second-largest eruption (of Mount Pinatubo) and a typhoon (Yunya) at the very same time! The eruption sent an ash cloud 22 miles (35 km) into the air, which combined with the typhoon's heavy rains to create lahars, very destructive flows of mud and ash. Waahh!

Much calmer now, I like to coo at my super-cute fauna. My adorable mouse deer, the chevrotain, tops the scales at just 17 pounds (7.5 kg). Can you smell buttered popcorn? That's just the natural aroma of my binturong, a slightly scruffy looking creature resembling a cross between a bear and a cat. My abacá trees produce a fiber known as Manila hemp; salt resistant, it's excellent for marine rope and fishing nets.

- **SIZE:** 115,831 sq mi (300,000 sq km)
- **POPULATION:** 102,624,000
- **CURRENCY:** Philippine peso
- **CAPITAL:** Manila
- **LANGUAGES:** Filipino, English

Indonesia

ASIA

* Indonesia has more than 100 active volcanoes; the best known is Krakatoa
* Deer Cave on Borneo has a bat population of some three million
* Lake Toba, in Sumatra, is the largest volcanic crater lake in the world

Island hop 'til you drop? You'll crash for sure if you try to visit all my islands: I've got around 17,000 of them, but only 8000 are inhabited. A beach bum center of the universe? Don't be fooled . . . there's much more at stake! I have the world's largest Muslim population and fourth-largest population overall. My people speak a staggering 300 languages between them.

High populations almost always equal deforestation: People burn down the jungle to create palm-oil plantations or simply to plant subsistence crops. What's a Javan slow loris to do? These primates live in the forest canopy. On my big island of Sumatra, the Sumatran tiger is hanging on by a claw: Paper companies want its habitat. Grrrr!

At least my native giant parasitic corpse flowers are doing well; their rotting-meat smell attracts flies, and that helps them get pollinated. Along with sweet-smelling jasmine and delicate moth orchids, they're my national flowers, but try putting all three in a bouquet . . . hmmm. Drumming is always good therapy, and that's where my gamelan orchestras of Java and Bali come in. The instruments, like the metallophone, are all played with mallets. Hammer away!

○ **SIZE:** 735,358 sq mi (1,904,569 sq km)
● **POPULATION:** 258,316,000
○ **CURRENCY:** Indonesian rupiah
● **CAPITAL:** Jakarta
○ **LANGUAGE:** Bahasa Indonesia

Island Life

Indonesia's main islands fall into several groups: The Greater Sunda Islands of Sumatra, Java, southern Borneo, and Celebes; the Lesser Sunda Islands, which include Bali; the Moluccas; and New Guinea.

Temple Territory

Thousands of temples dot the Indonesian landscape. In Java, the 10th-century Prambanan complex includes three ornately decorated temples dedicated to the three great Hindu divinities (Shiva, Vishnu, and Brahma). Pura Besakih, on the slopes of Mount Agung in Bali, features 23 temples.

Singapore

ASIA

* This cluster of small islands has two monsoon seasons: Nov–Mar and May–Sept
* Indigenous animals include slow lorises, long-tailed macaques, and scaly anteaters

- **SIZE:** 269 sq mi (697 sq km)
- **POPULATION:** 5,782,000
- **CURRENCY:** Singapore dollar
- **CAPITAL:** Singapore
- **LANGUAGES:** Mandarin, English, Malay, Tamil

A city-state at the southern tip of the Malay Peninsula, my low-elevation location has left me vulnerable to sea-level rise. It has also brought me great fortune. You see, my massive Port of Singapore sits at the mouth of the Malacca Strait, a stretch of water that has more than 40 percent of the world's sea traffic passing through it. I'm expert at the computer logistics needed to wrangle all that traffic, at maritime law, and ship brokerage. I've invested in some pretty eye-catching architecture—check out my lotus-blossom-shaped ArtScience Museum and my vertical gardens, which feature a grove of 18 solar-powered, energy-producing "super trees" that weave ferns and tropical plants into their branched steel structure. My famous half-lion/half-fish Merlion fountain at the mouth of the Singapore River symbolizes my status as a lion of the sea.

Brunei

ASIA

A diddy sovereign state on the north coast of Borneo, my land consists of two unconnected halves. Oil and gas have made me rich; the sultan's home, Istana Nurul Iman, is the largest residential palace in the world. You try finding your way around 1788 rooms, 257 bathrooms, and a stable for 200 polo ponies! In my lowland tropical rain forest, my proboscis monkey is easy to spot, with its 4-inch- (10-cm-) long hooter.

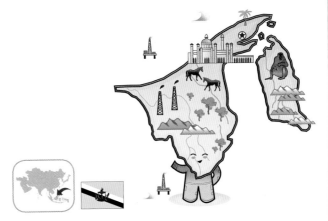

- **SIZE:** 2226 sq mi (5765 sq km)
- **POPULATION:** 437,000
- **CURRENCY:** Bruneian dollar
- **CAPITAL:** Bandar Seri Begawan
- **LANGUAGE:** Malay

East Timor

ASIA

G aining independence from Indonesia in 2002, I'm the 21st-century's first sovereign state. Rugged and mountainous, I form half of the island of Timor, home to hot springs and villages with thatch-roofed houses. Coffee, cinnamon, and cocoa love my tropical climate. Around me lie beautiful coral reefs with barracuda, dugongs, and reef sharks swimming in the clear waters. My national park protects wildlife, such as the endangered yellow-crested cockatoo.

- **SIZE:** 5743 sq mi (14,874 sq km)
- **POPULATION:** 1,261,000
- **CURRENCY:** U.S. dollar
- **CAPITAL:** Dili
- **LANGUAGES:** Tetum, Portuguese

Oceania

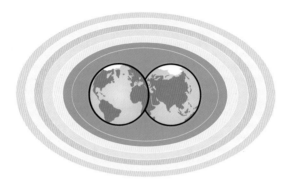

I've got more ground than you think—it's just that a lot of it is having a good long soak beneath the Pacific Ocean. A bathymetric map—that's a map showing underwater terrain—would tell the tale: New Zealand may look like two skinny islands bathing in the South Pacific, but that's just the bits that decided to get some fresh air. Idling beneath the waves is a land mass the size of India, known as Zealandia. My other major landmasses are Australia and New Guinea. What goes on underwater, though, doesn't always stay there: It's all about tectonic temper tantrums. When the deep layers of Earth get hot under the crusty collar, plates start crashing, supercontinents split up, and volcanic islands spit up from the ocean floor: My Melanesian islands are all volcanic.

* **Land mass:** 3,291,903 sq mi (8,525,989 sq km)
* **Number of countries:** 14

* **Biggest lake:** Eyre
* **Longest river:** Murray
* **Highest mountain:** Puncak Jaya

Oceania

Australia

Fiji

Kiribati

Marshall Islands

Micronesia

Nauru

New Zealand

Palau

Papua New Guinea

Samoa

Solomon Islands

Tonga

Tuvalu

Vanuatu

Marshall
Islands

Palau

Micronesia

Nauru

Kiribati

Pacific Ocean

Papua
New
Guinea

Solomon
Islands

Tuvalu

Samoa

*Coral
Sea*

Vanuatu

Fiji

Tonga

Australia

*Great
Australian Bight*

*Tasman
Sea*

New
Zealand

Southern Ocean

181

Australia

OCEANIA

* Sydney Opera House's roofline is shaped like a series of shimmering "sails"
* New South Wales lays claim to some of the world's best surfing beaches
* Tasmania's fragrant Huon pine trees can grow to be 2500 years old

My outback will always be upfront in my popular image, but there's more to me than rusty red dirt, salt scrub bushes, and kangaroos. Secluded in the South Pacific, I'm roamed by a good number of strange species that reflect my biodiversity. Echidnas and platypuses, for example, are the world's only monotremes (that's egg-laying mammals to you). My Great Dividing Range hugs the contours of my east coast and the ancient Flinders Ranges rise up in my south. In Western Australia and my Northern Territory, you'll find the world's two largest monoliths (massive rocks), Mount Augustus and Uluru (Ayer's Rock). For my native Aborigines, whose Dreaming stories revolve around the natural world, Uluru has long been held a sacred site.

Would you believe that almost 70 percent of my territory is desert and mostly low-lying? I'm also of two minds about trees: In my southwest, there's the Nullarbor Plain—the name means "no trees" in Latin—but in my Queensland province, I boast the Daintree—Earth's oldest tropical rain forest. The Nullarbor is the site of the 3420-mile- (5500-km-) long Great Barrier Fence: the world's longest, built to keep predatory dingoes away from sheep!

- **SIZE:** 2,988,902 sq mi (7,741,220 sq km)
- **POPULATION:** 22,993,000
- **CURRENCY:** Australian dollar
- **CAPITAL:** Canberra
- **LANGUAGE:** English

Bush Tucker

Bush tucker is Aussie speak for the country's nourishing native plants, berries, and fruits. They include riberries, muntries (great in chutnies), sandalwood nuts, cinnamon myrtle, and blood limes.

The Great Barrier Reef

The world's largest coral reef lies offshore of Queensland. Vast and colorful, it is home to 600 types of corals, 100 species of jellyfish, and 3000 different mollusks, sharks, rays, dolphins, and dugongs. Recent rises in sea temperatures have caused areas of the reef to die off.

New Zealand

OCEANIA

* Some 27 million sheep live in New Zealand; six for each member of the population
* Commercial bungee jumping is said to have originated in New Zealand
* Great Barrier Island is home to hot springs, where you can bathe

Very far away from anywhere else, I lie 930 miles (1500 km) southeast of Australia, separated by the Tasman Sea. Consider me top tramping territory! My North Island features mountains running down the center, with rich farmland on either side. Sheep love to graze here and are the source of my cozy New Zealand wool. My South Island's massive Southern Alps give way to Fiordland, which combines mountain, glacier, fjord, and rain-forest biomes! The Alps run onto a wide stretch called the Canterbury Plains, farmland formed by alluvial deposit—runoff from the mountains. Offshore, Stewart Island is home to penguins and my national bird, the kiwi.

My species evolved in total isolation out here, and so many of them are seriously strange—like *Powelliphanta*, an egg-laying, carnivorous snail that sucks up earthworms like spaghetti and can live up to 20 years. My native tuatara reptile has a third eye on top of its head that's like a clock—it helps know the time of day and the tuatara season!

I have urban attractions, too, such as Auckland's Sky Tower, which reaches 1076 feet (328 m) skyward—my tallest building. And, of course, there is the Beehive in Wellington. Part of my parliamentary complex, it looks . . . well, like a beehive!

- **SIZE:** 103,799 sq mi (268,838 sq km)
- **POPULATION:** 4,475,000
- **CURRENCY:** New Zealand dollar
- **CAPITAL:** Wellington
- **LANGUAGES:** English, Maori

Flightless Birds

New Zealand has the most species of flightless birds, including the kiwi and the penguin. Before humans, birds had no predators on land, and without any need to make an escape, they lost their ability to fly.

The Maoris

My native people call me Aotearoa, "Land of the Long White Cloud," for my misty mountain ranges. Polynesian people who first beached their canoes on my shores around 1000 C.E., Maoris are known for their *tamoko* (swirly tattoos) chiseled into the skin, and for the *haka*, a grunting and grimacing war dance.

Papua New Guinea

OCEANIA

- ✳ Each of the 700 Papuan and Melanesian tribes speaks its own language
- ✳ Asaro "mudmen" re-create warrior ancestors wearing huge mud masks

○ **SIZE:** 178,704 sq mi
  (462,840 sq km)

◐ **POPULATION:**
  6,791,000

○ **CURRENCY:**
  Papua New Guinean kina

● **CAPITAL:**
  Port Moresby

○ **LANGUAGES:**
  Tok Pisin, English,
  Hiri Motu

Is that a crocodile tickling my toes? My 30,000-square-mile (80,000-sq-km), largely unexplored Sepik River basin is known for tribes who hunt crocodiles. They submerge themselves in river vegetation and rummage in the mud with their bare hands and feet!

A resource-rich land covered by rain and cloud forests, I have a central mountain range—the Highlands—and at least 100 volcanoes.

But lava is not the only danger here. Growing 6 feet (1.8 m) tall, my blue-necked cassowary, a bird, can deliver a nasty blow with its lethal, daggerlike claw. Better to stick with my spotted cuscus, a cat-sized, ginger-dappled possum. My Anga tribespeople mummify respected elders in a complex smoking ritual and place them on cliffs overlooking their villages as a comforting link to the world of ancestor spirits.

Marshall Islands

OCEANIA

My territory includes many scattered islands, but also atolls. These rings of land around lagoons are the scant remains of extinct volcanoes. You might have heard of my atoll Bikini, which means land of the coconuts. Its name was adopted by a French fashion designer for a teeny two-piece swimming suit. But be careful if you swim in my waters; I have the world's largest shark sanctuary—four times the size of California.

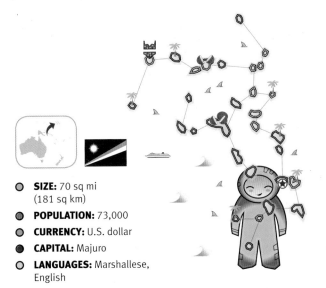

- **SIZE:** 70 sq mi (181 sq km)
- **POPULATION:** 73,000
- **CURRENCY:** U.S. dollar
- **CAPITAL:** Majuro
- **LANGUAGES:** Marshallese, English

Palau

OCEANIA

Saltwater crocodiles lounge in the mangrove swamps of my hot and rainy islands. You might also see crab-eating macaques. Locals picnic by the monolithic stones at Badrulchau, on my Babeldaob Island, and divers plunge into pristine waters around my coral reefs and wartime shipwrecks. At Koror, you can swim with trained dolphins at Dolphin Pacific, the largest dolphin research center in the world.

- **SIZE:** 177 sq mi (459 sq km)
- **POPULATION:** 21,000
- **CURRENCY:** U.S. dollar
- **CAPITAL:** Ngerulmud
- **LANGUAGES:** Palauan, English

Kiribati

OCEANIA

Straddling the Equator, and the international date line, my Millennium Island is the first place in the world to celebrate New Year. Getting to many of my white-sand beaches involves sailing there. Try a Kiribati canoe, built traditionally without using screws or nails. The Phoenix Island Protected Area is the largest marine conservation site in the world; see if you can spot the endangered Phoenix petrel, just one of my many seabirds.

- **SIZE:** 313 sq mi (811 sq km)
- **POPULATION:** 107,000
- **CURRENCY:** Kiribati dollar
- **CAPITAL:** Tarawa
- **LANGUAGES:** Gilbertese, English

Micronesia

OCEANIA

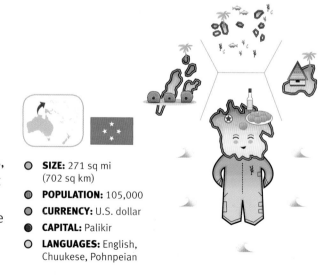

My many islands make up four states whose traditional meeting houses have high pointed roofs. On the island of Yap, huge stones called Rai have holes carved in the middle and once acted as currency. You might enjoy green tangerines, whereas *sakau*, a drink made from the root of the kava plant, is an acquired taste. My largest city is on Chuuk Lagoon where more than 250 fish varieties swim among 80 coral-encrusted World War II shipwrecks.

- **SIZE:** 271 sq mi (702 sq km)
- **POPULATION:** 105,000
- **CURRENCY:** U.S. dollar
- **CAPITAL:** Palikir
- **LANGUAGES:** English, Chuukese, Pohnpeian

Samoa

OCEANIA

- ✳ Extensive body tattoos are considered a mark of man- or womanhood
- ✳ Staple foods include *copra* (dried coconut), cocoa beans, and bananas

- **SIZE:** 1093 sq mi (2831 sq km)
- **POPULATION:** 199,000
- **CURRENCY:** Samoan tala
- **CAPITAL:** Apia
- **LANGUAGE:** Samoan

Welcome to my small archipelago dominated by two large central South Pacific islands. I am the product of ancient volcanic activity; today only my westernmost Savai'i island boasts live volcanoes: Mata o le Afi, Mount Matavanu, and Mauga Afi.

Hungry for a coral palolo worm or two? This seasonal delicacy rises to the sea surface just once a year to spawn, only to be netted and noshed on the spot by locals! My Teuila Festival, named for my red ginger flowers, celebrates Fa'a Samoa, or the Samoan way. Events include *fa'ataupati*, an all-male dance that imitates the gyrations used to smack my voracious mosquitoes. Mosquitoes aside, Europeans find me an island paradise: Robert Louis Stevenson, author of *Treasure Island* and *Kidnapped*, spent his happiest years on my large island, Upolu.

Tonga

OCEANIA

My archipelago stretches some 500 miles (800 km), but most people live on Tongatapu, home to the royal palace. You might see a flying fox here—actually it is a bat and considered sacred, or *tabu* (the origin of the word "taboo"). Tongans like to eat, and their feasts may consist of dozens of dishes, particularly suckling pig and steamed fish. Obesity has traditionally been seen as attractive, but men must keep their shirts on in public.

- **SIZE:** 288 sq mi (747 sq km)
- **POPULATION:** 107,000
- **CURRENCY:** Tongan Pa'anga
- **CAPITAL:** Nuku'alofa
- **LANGUAGES:** Tongan, English

Fiji

OCEANIA

Tourists visit me for my romantic white beaches; honeymooners head for my island resorts with thatched-roofed huts called *bure*. Covered in forests, my tropical islands are producers of sugar cane, coconuts, and copra. Elsewhere, you'll find cane toads, iguanas, geckos, and turtles among my reptiles. Fijians are hooked on rugby, and the national team is known for performing a *Cibi*, a traditional war dance, before a match.

- **SIZE:** 7056 sq mi (18,274 sq km)
- **POPULATION:** 915,000
- **CURRENCY:** Fijian dollar
- **CAPITAL:** Suva
- **LANGUAGES:** English, Fijian, Hindi

Solomon Islands

OCEANIA

* Lake Tegano, on Rennell Island, is the largest of all Pacific Island lakes
* A WWII shipwreck breaks through the surface of the sea north of Honiara

- **SIZE:** 11,157 sq mi (28,896 sq km)
- **POPULATION:** 635,000
- **CURRENCY:** Solomon Islands dollar
- **CAPITAL:** Honiara
- **LANGUAGES:** English, Melanesian Pidgin

Defending biodiversity is my passion—it would have to be, given my six large and nearly 1000 small islands. My Arnavon island group is a major nesting site for hawksbill sea turtles: Every year, my sand skitters as hundreds of little hatchlings scramble their way out of nests and head for the sea. My cozy, warm volcanic sand serves as a babysitter for the megapode, or incubator bird, who lays its eggs in thermal sand burrows, so the mother doesn't have to sit on a nest. My money was once made of bird feathers: fiber coils wrapped in red feathers from the scarlet honeyeater.

The children from my islands are expert canoers: Who needs a bicycle when you've got an outrigger canoe and plenty of lagoons to paddle through? At sundown, music sounds from pan pipes, or bamboo flutes, and slit drums.

Nauru

OCEANIA

I'm tiny—you can walk around me in a few hours, admiring the coral pinnacles off my coast. And I'm exhausted, too. You see, phosphates—seabird droppings that once made me the second-richest country in the world—are all but mined out now. Seabirds still come here, though, to rest on their long flights: Noddies are caught and eaten, and frigate birds are trapped and tamed. I'm not far from Australia, and Australian-rules football is my most popular sport.

- **SIZE:** 8 sq mi (21 sq km)
- **POPULATION:** 10,000
- **CURRENCY:** Australian dollar
- **CAPITAL:** Yaren
- **LANGUAGES:** Nauruan, English

Vanuatu

OCEANIA

Forgive me if my tummy rumbles . . . earthquakes and volcanoes, such as the dramatic Yasur on my island of Tanna, often shake my archipelago. No wonder many reality-TV survivor programs have been set here! I am hot and rainy nine months of the year, so scuba divers find my waters warm and welcoming. Horseback riding is popular, too. Cattle are my most important livestock, though pigs are considered a sign of wealth—more so if they have tusks.

- **SIZE:** 4,706 sq mi (12,189 sq km)
- **POPULATION:** 278,000
- **CURRENCY:** Vanuatu vatu
- **CAPITAL:** Port Vila
- **LANGUAGES:** Bislama, French, English

Tuvalu

OCEANIA

* Te Ano is a national game—a little like volleyball; it has two balls in play at a time
* Tuvaluan women make jewelry from cowrie (sea-snail) shells

Remote? I've heard that word before. It's true, you'll squint to see me on a map of the South Pacific, riding the waves about 2500 miles (4000 km) northeast of Australia. My name means "eight standing together," for my eight low-lying atolls, none more than 15 feet (4.5 m) above sea level. Flooding is a real problem. My people know their land could be submerged, and they've taken the initiative to reduce dependence on imported diesel and increase use of wind and solar for power instead.

Weird, but fresh water can be a problem here, too, because there are no rivers—so rainfall is crucial. My only native mammal is a rat. Sure, you'll see chickens, goats, pigs, and dogs, but they are all imported. My people are mostly subsistence farmers, growing coconut palms, breadfruit trees, and bananas. The rate of fish consumption here is one of the world's highest—duh! Tuvaluans fish from hand-crafted canoes, using butterfly nets to catch flying fish.

- **SIZE:** 10 sq mi (26 sq km)
- **POPULATION:** 11,000
- **CURRENCY:** Tuvaluan or Australian dollar
- **CAPITAL:** Funafuti
- **LANGUAGES:** Tuvaluan, English

193

Glossary

Annex—to take control of a region or country and make it part of another region or country.

Archipelago—a group of neighboring islands and/or islets within the same body of water.

Arid—dry, barren.

Atoll—a ring-shaped coral reef, island, or group of islets surrounding a lagoon.

Autonomous—independent, self-governing.

Biodiversity—the variety of life-forms within a particular habitat, ecosystem, or country.

Biome—a community of plants and animals living in a particular physical environment.

Camel caravan—traders or tribespeople riding a line of camels packed with trade goods or possessions across a desert landscape.

Cassava—a tropical plant cultivated for its root; cassava flour (for bread), tapioca pudding, and even laundry starch are made from the root.

Cataract—a large waterfall that falls over a precipice as opposed to falling over rocks.

Civil war—a war between groups of people who are citizens of the same country.

Colony—a country or region under the political control of another, usually distant, country.

Communisim—a political system in which major resources such as mines, factories, and farms are owned by the state, and wealth is divided equally among citizens.

Delta—an area of wetlands that forms at the mouth of a river, where it empties into a larger body of water.

El Niño—an irregularly occurring flow of unusually warm surface water off the western coast of South America that disrupts normal weather patterns.

Elevation—the distance of an area of land above sea level.

Emirate—an area ruled by an emir—a type of leader—in some Islamic countries.

Epicenter—the very central point of something; especially, the location where the greatest damage from an earthquake occurs.

Erosion—the wearing away of material, such as earth or rock, by the constant flow of water or wind.

EU—European Union; association of European nations formed in 1993 to promote political and economic integration.

Export—to sell, or transport for sale, goods and services outside the country in which the goods or services are produced.

Fauna—the native animals of a given region.

Federation—a central political authority formed by smaller groups (such as countries, states, or counties) that give up some individual power to the federation.

Fertile—describes rich soil or land that is able to produce abundant crops.

Fjord—a long, narrow inlet of the sea surrounded by steep cliffs, common in Norway and Iceland; usually cut by glaciers.

Fortification—a defensive wall, moat, bank, or fort; a construction built for defense.

Fumarole—a vent in Earth's surface that releases hot vapor, steam, and/or gases.

Geothermal power—heat from Earth's interior converted into an energy source, such as steam used to power a turbine generator.

Glacier—a large ice mass that moves very slowly over land.

Hominid—a primate mammal that stands erect on two feet; hominids include humans, human ancestors, and some great apes.

Hydroelectric power—electrical power produced through the use of the gravitational force of flowing water.

Indigenous—originating in, or native to, a particular place.

Irrigation—supplying water by artificial means: for example, watering a field by underground water piping.

Karst—an area of land formed from dissolvable rock, such as limestone, usually featuring underground drainage systems with sinkholes and caves.

Lagoon—a shallow body of saltwater separated from the ocean by sand bars, barrier islands, or coral reefs.

Landlocked—a country almost, or entirely, surrounded by land; having no coastline.

Latrine—a very basic toilet.

Magma—molten rock usually located deep beneath Earth's crust that occasionally comes to the surface through cracks in the crust or through the eruption of volcanoes.

Mangroves—salt-tolerant tropical trees with densely tangled, aboveground root systems; they help to stabilize coastlines by protecting them from flooding.

Marsupial—a mammal that bears immature babies, then carries them in a belly pouch.

Mesa—an isolated flat-topped hill with steep sides.

Mineral—a material that is neither animal nor plant, and which makes up Earth's rocks, soils, and sands.

Migratory—describes animals or people who move from one place to another for work, grazing, weather, or to reach better economic or survival conditions.

Mineral ore—a natural deposit of a mineral in rock, from which metal can be extracted, for example cassiterite (an ore of tin).

Mono-cropping—growing the same crop every year on the same land; the opposite of crop rotation; often reduces soil fertility.

Monsoon—usually in Southeast Asia, a reversal in the direction of the prevailing (strongest) winds that brings heavy rainfall.

NATO—a pact formed in 1949 by many North American and European nations, providing for mutual defense if a member nation is attacked.

Nomadic—having no fixed home; often native tribes who migrate according to seasons for better grazing or hunting and gathering.

Oasis—a small fertile area in the middle of a desert, with a water source, such as a spring.

Outpost—a settlement, town, or camp that is established far away from the center of things.

Paleolithic—of or relating to the time during the early Stone Age when people made rough tools and weapons out of stone; about 2 to 2.5 million years ago.

Pastoral—describes activities related to livestock raising and people whose occupation is herding livestock.

Peninsula—a piece of land almost entirely surrounded by water but connected to the mainland on one side.

Petroglyph—an image or symbol (usually prehistoric) carved into rock.

Plain—a large, flat area of land with few trees.

Plateau—an area of high, level ground.

Poacher—a person who kills wildlife illegally to sell to others.

Porous—easy to pass through; especially, a material full of pores (holes) that allow air or water to travel through.

Prairie—a large, open grassland region.

Primate—a member of a highly developed mammal group, including humans, monkeys, gorillas, and chimpanzees.

Primeval—of, or relating to, earliest times.

Promontory—a high point of land or rock that projects into a body of water.

Rain shadow—an area of land that is desert because mountains block rainy weather.

Renewable—something (often an energy source) that is not depleted (used up, destroyed) when used.

Salt flat—a salt-encrusted area of land, often formed as a result of evaporation of a former body of water.

Savanna—grassy tropical or subtropical plain.

Shaman—a priest or priestess who acts as a go-between between the mortal and spirit worlds.

Sirocco—a hot dry wind blowing from North Africa and affecting southern Europe.

Soviet Union—Union of Soviet Socialist Republics, from 1922 to 1991, a one-party Communist state.

Supercontinent—an ancient large continent or landmass thought to have consisted of modern continents before they broke apart.

Sustainable—a method of harvesting that prevents a resource becoming depleted or permanently damaged.

Tabletop mountain—a flat-topped, steep-sided mountain.

Taiga—a coniferous forest in high northern latitudes dominated by fir and spruce trees.

Tectonic plate—a sub-layer of Earth's crust that moves, floats, and sometimes fractures, and whose movement causes continental drift, earthquakes, volcanoes, and mountains.

Terrain—the physical features of land, such as hills, valleys, rocky ledges, forested areas, and streams.

Topography—the physical or natural features of a landscape.

Tundra—a vast, flat, treeless Arctic region of Europe, Asia, and North America, in which the subsoil is permanently frozen.

Typhoon—both typhoon and hurricane are regional terms for tropical cyclones.

Voodoo—a religion that believes all natural things, living or not, have souls that can influence worldy events.

Weathering—the natural effects of time and the elements on an object, person, or place.

Index

Numbers in **bold** indicate country entries